February 1994

Eileen —

Warm regards,
and happy paddling —

Dick Squire

Eileen E Sordi
22 Harbor Heights Dr
Centerport, NY 11721-1621

How to play Platform Tennis

How to play
Platform
Tennis

BY DICK SQUIRES

Trade books distributed by:
National Book Network
Lanham, MD

Published by Squirrel Publishing Co.,
326 Rowayton Avenue,
Rowayton, CT 06853

LC# 76-79381
ISBN: 0-9635285-5-6

Photographs by Jim Herity
Book design by Kathleen Burke

Frontispiece

Tom Glover is a longtime friend and neighbor of mine in Rowayton, Conn. He is an extraordinarily adept caricaturist possessing that unique ability to capture both the likeness and essence of a person "on canvas" in just about three minutes.

His artistic talents won him a five-year assignment of drawing celebs and guests attending R.J. Nabisco/PGA Tour golf events. He estimates he has sketched more than 100,000 people since 1978 when he started to specialize in corporate caricaturing.

Tom and I are presently collaborating on another literary project, but I wanted him to make a (free) contribution to this new version of the old HOW TO PLAY PLATFORM TENNIS. On the facing page is what he created. Although it hurts, oddly enough I like it!

Re-writing this book has, in fact, rejuvenated me both physically and mentally. It has also re-awakened my fondness for this marvelous sport and the nice people who play it.

Foreword

I asked Gerri Viant to review this book and write a few lines about what she thought. She read it over a weekend and was on the phone early Monday morning. "It's good," she exclaimed. "I just hope you've changed your earlier views on mixed doubles."

I assured her I had. In re-reading the old chapter on mixed doubles one could interpret some of my words as being mean, as well as demeaning, when describing women and their on-court role. While the chauvinistic attitude exhibited in my 30s has mellowed with age, the real enlightenment has occurred because the distaffers have improved immensely.

In order to obtain a new batch of photographs for this edition, I accompanied my photographer to the National Mixed and National Men's and Women's Doubles Championships in the spring of 1992. It had been almost a decade since I had watched the top women play. They were wonderful!

Placated, Gerri agreed to go ahead and critique the book. Here is what she wrote.

I am thrilled to see an updated version of Dick Squires' classic book on platform tennis. While the basic principles and strokes have remained the same, the game has been enhanced by younger, fitter tennis players who have taken up paddle. Improved equipment has brought about changes. These factors have contributed to a faster, more aggressive style of play that has accelerated the sport to another, higher level.

Dick has acknowledged the evolution during the past 20 years, and particularly the progress that has occurred in women's play. In this revised edition he has written a comprehensive and current book that can be enjoyed by players of all skill levels.

As a teaching professional and player, I can fully understand why thousands of paddle players of all ages, beginners as well as advanced, have enjoyed earlier printings of this little instructional gem. This updated version is the best ever!

Gerri Viant

Gerri came to the United States from Australia. She is presently the tennis/paddle pro and manager of the Nyack Field Club in Nyack, N.Y. She was National Women's Champion in 1988,'90 and '92, and National Mixed Doubles titleholder in 1989.

She served as a director of the APTA from 1988 to 1990 and is currently on the Vittert pro staff assisting them in new-product development.

Contents

Acknowledgements

Thanks to my wife, Doc, who encouraged me to self-publish HOW TO PLAY PLATFORM TENNIS. "It's going to be a winner," she kept reminding me as I worked on the manuscript until the wee hours of many mornings.

Thanks to Marcraft's Duffy Lautz who first suggested the idea of republishing the book. "The sport's coming back and the timing is right," he assured me.

Thanks to Kathy Burke, the lovely and talented Art Director of TENNIS USTA. When I asked her to design the book she said she'd love to.

Thanks to the skillful "models" who gave up a good part of a beautiful spring day to be photographed on court for some of the instructional pictures: Jay Packer, Connie Jones and my son, Gary.

And, finally, thanks to whomever it was who invited me out onto a paddle court for the first time back in the early 1960s. I am truly indebted to that person for introducing me to a wonderful pastime.

Dedication

This updated version of the original "little green book" is dedicated to all platform tennis players and aficionados, past, present and future. You are all a unique and enjoyable breed. This wonderful sport seems to attract the rare likes of you!

About the author

When the first printing of "the little green book," HOW TO PLAY PLATFORM TENNIS, was published (1969), its author, Dick Squires, instantly became known as "Mr. Platform Tennis."

He was a good player, a fiery competitor, and obviously had a lot of fun on (and off) the court. It was this book, however, that established him as an "authority" on the game.

Not only was it the first book that explained the basic strokes, strategies and tactics, but the straightforward, simplistic style in which it was written was what made it a "best seller."

HOW TO PLAY PLATFORM TENNIS was bought by 25,000 paddlers (five printings) of all skill levels. In 1977, the McGraw-Hill Book Company purchased the softcover rights from the original publisher, Devin Adair Company.

During the decade of the 1970s Squires became involved in all aspects of the game. His company, Sports Marketing Associates Corp., built courts all over the country. His signature appeared on paddles, shoes, balls, gloves and sweaters, even a line of playing attire that sported a squirrel logo.

He promoted unique tournaments and cajoled companies into sponsoring monied events that were shown on national television. He was the "expert" commentator behind the microphone. To inaugurate new courts, he played in "hundreds" of exhibitions.

Houghton Mifflin published THE COMPLETE BOOK OF PLATFORM TENNIS (1973), which Squires conceived and edited. In 1978 THE <u>OTHER</u> RACQUET SPORTS was published (McGraw-Hill) in which Squires covered the origin, appeal and methods of play for all racquet and paddle games (other than tennis), from court tennis to pickle-ball.

Since 1983 Dick Squires has been affiliated with THE NEW YORK TIMES' sports and leisure magazine division. He is publisher of two magazines, TENNIS BUYER'S GUIDE and TENNIS USTA. This position affords him the opportunity to do what he enjoys most: selling, promoting and writing.

Many years ago, tennis' Bill Tilden wrote MATCH PLAY AND SPIN OF THE BALL, and golf's Bobby Jones penned ON GOLF. Both books are still in print and are selling well today. They are deemed to be true, timeless "classics" on their respective sports.

This updated version of "the definitive book on platform tennis," authored by an individual who has played them all well enough to win national titles in three different racquet sports, is indeed worthy of the same cherished "classic" consideration and recognition.

Introduction

How did this updated version of HOW TO PLAY PLATFORM TENNIS come about? Who in his right mind would want to read words that were written more than 23 years ago? And, while the author still plays in club-league competition—at 61—he cannot move around "the boards" as quickly as he could when the first printing of the book was published in 1969.

Here is what happened. Duffy Lautz, president of Marcraft Recreation Corp., the company that has manufactured most of the game's paddles for as long as I can remember, called me in the fall of 1991 and advised me that the sport was evidencing a resurgence in popularity. It wasn't so everywhere but in specific geographical "pockets." He thought the "timing was right" for a new printing of "the classic, little green book that thousands of paddle players were brought up on a generation ago."

He then reminded me that Bill Tilden's "MATCH PLAY AND THE SPIN OF THE BALL," plus Bobby Jones' "ON GOLF" were classics and would be published and read as long as tennis and golf were popular pastimes.

Then Duffy clinched it. "They were the 'masters' in their respective sports. You were the master in platform tennis. . ."

"Say no more, Duff," I said. "You really know how to handle me. If you feel you can sell some copies, I'll do the rewrite."

That's the honest-to-goodness scenario. He felt there was a need for an updated paddle primer and that I was the guy who could write it, if only from memory.

You want to know something? As I started the rewrite process, I found out quickly that there were few concepts and words that had changed. What was penned more than two decades ago still, for the most part, holds true today.

Because the majority of the top players on the present-day tour are younger and better athletes than "in my day," play has become somewhat more aggressive. A marked improvement in paddle construction and a better ball have affected play and strategy somewhat. But not a heck of a lot.

Each chapter is prefaced with an Author's Note that reflects my present thinking about the particular subject being presented. If my thoughts written 20 years ago have changed, or remained unaltered, they are expressed in the italicized Author's Note.

The bottom line, however, is that the sport really has not changed much. Because there are so many equalizers—the screens, small court, high net, single serve—placement, patience, and consistency will almost always win out over power, speed of foot and low-percentage shots.

That is why the "old guys" can still hold their own, even win occasionally, when up against some lean and mean youngsters. That is the beauty of this wonderful game. That is why this "old guy" can still write with credibility on the basic strokes and strategies of the sport.

Dick Squires, November, 1992

A word about right- and left-handers

In all cases, unless otherwise noted, the text dealing with the basic paddle strokes and strategies is written for a right-handed platform tennis player. A southpaw will have to keep this in mind as he/she reads and attempts to follow and practice the principles recommended in this book.

It has also been assumed that the reader's opponents are right-handed.

Because of the increasing number of lefties playing the game, however, a few comments have been included specifically for their benefit.

I hope the women will forgive me for usually employing male gender terms when describing the players (he, him). It is just less cumbersome to do so.

Finally, when talking about the left or right side of the court, I am referring to that side as seen from *across the net.* In other words, the left side of the rival's court is the forehand (or deuce) side and the right side is the backhand (ad) court.

chapter 1
The birth of platform tennis, and up to the present

A uthor's Note: Twenty years ago I thought this marvelous game could and would become every bit as popular as tennis. Why not? It has appeals that both male and female adults and youngsters can truly enjoy for a lifetime.

The court consumes one-quarter of the area of a tennis court and can be installed practically anywhere.

Also, it can be played in <u>any</u> kind of weather.

All pluses, right?

Unfortunately, I no longer believe the game will match tennis in popularity. Why? Primarily because the cost of constructing a court has gone up so prodigiously in recent years.

Yes, the aluminum court is a bonafide advancement, but it also skyrocketed the price tag.

If people living in warmer climates discovered paddle, courts could be built like mini-tennis courts on ground level. Because there is little or no snowfall, there would be no need to elevate the deck. The playing surface could also be similar to what is used on so-called hard tennis courts. A superstructure could easily be erected around the 30'x60' playing area, and the complete installation would be drastically reduced.

But, and it's a big but, the "catch" is to get the game going in warm-weather areas. That means going

*against the tradition of the sport, and that can be a
hard sell!*

While other racquet games such as tennis and squash have foreign roots (England), and their origins go back several hundred years, platform tennis, or affectionately called "paddle," and erroneously called "paddle tennis," had its beginnings about 64 years ago in the New York City suburb of Scarsdale, N.Y. It's as American as apple pie, baseball and maple syrup.

During the winter of 1928, a group of men who loved to play tennis decided to build an all-purpose recreational deck outside above the snow level that would provide them with a weekend, outdoor playing field during the dreary, cold months. Indoor tennis, in those days, was confined to dimly lit armories and gymnasiums on lightning-quick, highly polished wooden floors.

The original deck (or platform) was intended for the playing of deck tennis (a popular pastime on cruiser ships), badminton and volleyball. The "Father" of platform tennis, Fessenden Blanchard, joined his close pal, James K. Cogswell, in erecting the elevated solid deck in the latter's backyard. Before the end of the winter other friends and neighbors came in on the work and fun.

The group became known as "The Old Army Athletes," not because they were all war veterans, but because Cogswell's home was located on historic Old Army Road. Upon completion of the wooden deck, eight-foot high chicken wire was installed around the perimeter to keep the ball in the playing area and neighborhood dogs out.

One Sunday morning Cogswell showed up with

some paddles and sponge rubber balls that were being used for a game played on the streets and playgrounds of New York City. It was called "paddle tennis." The paddle was square, had no holes and was fairly lightweight (eight-ounces). With these rather crude implements they began playing a game utilizing the same rules and scoring as tennis. Other intended sports were quickly discarded as the playing platform proved to be perfectly suited for a paddle and ball activity.

Because the deck was approximately 25 percent the area of a tennis court, they soon discovered (as do all newcomers to platform tennis) that the rallies were extended and it was quite difficult to put the ball away. There was a lot of activity in a confined space, and even the most out-of-shape gentleman had little difficulty covering his side of the court. It was fun and proved to be salubrious outdoor exercise during the frigid, dank days of winter.

How did playing balls off the wires evolve? Like most great inventions, by accident. The story goes that during a long rally a ball hit across the net landed fairly within the playing lines, then collided with the wire mesh screening and stuck there. Blanchard ran outside the court and smacked the ball with his paddle. It dislodged and soared across the net between his startled opponents. He claimed the point because the ball had not bounced a second time on the deck.

Thus was born the game's most unique (and fun) characteristic–returning balls "off the wires." Right then and there the athletes all agreed that the ball was still in play if it bounced fairly within the court lines then into the back or side screening, providing it was returned before striking the deck a second time.

During that winter another unique rule was

3

devised. The players decided to allow only one serve, which eliminated the big advantage a strong server had. (This might be something the various tennis associations should consider!) It also speeded up play and introduced some added pressure into the game.

Other Scarsdale people living in the area dropped by to see them play, then tried it themselves. This "bastard" form of mini-tennis produced many pleasant hours of exhilarating exercise during the weekends for these weekday, sedentary train commuters to New York City. Wives joined in on the fun and they, too, realized they could hold up their own side of the court even better than on a tennis court.

Soon a new deck was erected at the Cogswells'. The playing area was reduced slightly to 30'x60', and the playing lines painted down were the same dimensions as badminton, 20'x44'. The back and side screening were raised from eight to 10 feet and eventually to the present height of 12 feet.

Most of the Old Army Athletes were tennis-playing members of the venerable Fox Meadow Club, which was located just about a mile from the Cogswell residence. In the fall of 1931, during the depths of the Depression, they approached the club's board members with the idea of installing a platform tennis court on the grounds. The concept was to provide an activity during the winter months that would keep the facility open and used year-round. This meant much-needed, additional revenues.

After some debate, it was agreed that a court could be erected "providing a backboard was built at one end of the court to allow for tennis practice." The first club court in the country was subsequently built at Fox Meadow in November 1931 for the nominal price of $400.

4

By then the rules of play had been well-established, as were the dimensions of the court. An important innovation had also been created by an engineer, Donald K. Evans. He redesigned the backstop (now called the superstructure) so that the one-inch, wire-mesh screening would be suspended away from the uprights and could be stretched tightly and set under even-tension. The problem of irregular bounces was, for the most part, resolved.

The new sport caught the fancy of other area clubs. Installations were made at private homes with strict adherence to the plans drawn up by Blanchard. The Old Army Athletes apparently did a great job of promoting and selling their newfound love.

The first "official" platform tennis tournament on record was held at Fox Meadow in December 1931. Forty-two teams competed in the championship, which was, appropriately, won by Fessenden Blanchard and his friend, James Hynson.

Fox Meadow Club began to experience some prosperity due directly to increased interest in "paddle." Many members joined specifically to play the new "paddle and ball game." The first platforms built at nearby clubs were erected on top of the tennis courts. They went up in the fall and were dismantled in the spring. Eventually, however, as the game grew and became more popular, permanent structures were constructed in open, unutilized areas on the club grounds.

After a short time, adjoining communities heard about the game that had become so popular in Scarsdale. The Manursing Island Club in Rye, N.Y., had some addicts, and in 1932 two courts were put in. Soon a friendly, but intense rivalry began between these two suburban clubs and interclub competition was born. In 1934, sand was added to the paint used for the deck coating, which helped facilitate sure-footing even in the most inclement weather.

The American Paddle Tennis Association was founded and organized in 1934, and Blanchard became its first president. The Charter Club members included Fox Meadow, Manursing Island Club and the Field Club of Greenwich (Conn.). The name of the association (as well as the name of the sport) was formally and officially changed in 1950 to the American Platform Tennis Association (APTA).

Unfortunately even today, 40-plus years later, most players insist on calling it paddle tennis. The actual game of paddle tennis is still played in New York City, and a slightly different version has really caught on out on the West Coast. It is played with wooden paddles and punctured tennis balls on a ground-level, hard playing surface. The main difference between paddle tennis and platform tennis, however, is "playing the wires." That is the true essence and enjoyment of platform tennis! The mission of the APTA was (and still is) to standardize the equipment and playing rules and to promote the sport.

In 1935, the first "national" championships were staged at the founding club, Fox Meadow. Men's singles, men's and women's doubles and mixed-doubles tournaments were played. After only three years, the singles competition was dropped because the game was far more suited for doubles. (In recent years singles has been reintroduced with national events being held once again.)

The sport rapidly spread to Connecticut and New Jersey, and in 1936 a couple of upstart New Jerseyites, Harold Holmes and Dick Newell, walked off with the national crown in a marathon five-set match, 3-6, 8-6,

4-6, 9-7, 15-13 (thank God for tiebreakers!).

By 1940, just prior to World War II, the sport was being played quite extensively at clubs and on private backyard courts in the tri-state region of New York, New Jersey and Connecticut. While war-time gas rationing did cut down on interclub league play, and women's and mixed-doubles national tournaments were discontinued between 1943 and 1945, the men's doubles title was played for each year in the spring.

So much for the origin and "ancient" history of platform tennis. Suffice it to say that the sport, the court and the equipment evolved and improved over the years in similar fashion to tennis and squash racquets.

In the late 1960s, Richard J. Reilly developed the all-aluminum court structure that offered its owners, as an added accessory, a heated deck. Some wonderful traditions of paddle became passé. No longer would the first foursome on the court have to shovel and sweep off newly fallen snow. Warped 2"x6" Douglas fir wooden planks became outmoded. Bad bounces, usually on crucial points, were eliminated. It did take awhile, however, to become accustomed to the clangy, metallic sound of the ball hitting the playing surface.

The sport really began to spread and flourish in the early '70s. It became the "in" game in many pockets of the country. Some municipalities installed public parks courts. A few wealthy alumni donated structures to their alma maters in an effort to encourage youngsters to play. Commercial "pay-for-play" platform tennis centers sprang up in many locations, but all were destined to fail financially.

Why? The "paddle season" (approximately 32 weeks) was just too short. Inclement weather rained, snowed or iced out precious, never-to-be-recovered court time and revenues. Having to round up four people of about equal skill levels in order to have a good game became onerous. The tennis boom of the mid-'70s also sidetracked the popularization of paddle—particularly the construction of modern, well-lighted and posh indoor tennis facilities where people could play and be comfortable in cold-weather areas all winter long. The so-called "yummy mummies" (nonworking, middle-aged females) "made" these tennis clubs. They were the ones booking the courts during the day.

In addition, the construction costs of installed platform tennis courts became prohibitive, especially for towns and cities where the local parks and recreation department is always strapped for funds.

In 1973 two significant, landmark tournament events took place. For the first time in 38 years the Men's Nationals moved out of Fox Meadow to Cleveland—a definite sign that the game was beginning to spread out of the tri-state area. The same year I organized and promoted a tournament that had a lot of "firsts" attached to it. It was the first competitive paddle event staged in the south (Hilton Head Island, S.C.), the first one played for money ($10,000), the first with a commercial sponsor (Vat 69 Gold Scotch-National Distillers), and the first one shown (tape delayed) on nationwide television (CBS "Sports Spectacular").

By the mid-1970s, it was estimated there were 3,000 courts located in 39 states and some 300,000 players in the U.S. (In looking back I would say this figure was about as accurate as the A.C. Nielson's 1975 estimate of 36 million tennis players. Both numbers were most likely 50 percent higher than actuality.)

The APTA boasted of 265 member clubs, and an isolated number of courts had been erected in 10 foreign countries, including one at the American embassy in Moscow. So much activity was going on that the APTA opened up its own office and hired a paid executive director. I made several trips to Ireland, England, Belgium and France to promote the game and build some courts. The game was really humming!

The white ball that the Old Army Athletes originally employed had been changed to an orange/red ball in 1963. It was easier to see against a snowy backdrop. Ten years later, optic-yellow balls replaced the orange because they showed up better under the lights during night play.

Due to the apparent growth of the sport, the exposure it had been getting and the type of people playing the game (upscale, well educated and well heeled), Coca Cola Bottling Company of New York and Tribuno Wines became the corporate sponsors of the first professional platform tennis tour at the start of the 1975 season. Former tennis tour pros like Clark Graebner, Gene Scott and Herb FitzGibbon were attracted to the game. A team could pocket a few thousand dollars, plus have a lot of fun, over the course of a weekend.

The finals of the "Tribuno World Championships" were not played at Fox Meadow. Two temporary courts were installed at the historic tennis arena, Forest Hills, and spectators paid money to watch the top teams play platform tennis. The game had, at long last, in the winter of 1976, apparently come of age.

I happened to be doing the "expert commentary" for the telecast, along with TENNIS WEEK'S Gene Scott. He had been the announcer for the famous (or infamous) 1973 tennis confrontation between Billie

Jean King and Bobby Riggs. Many sports historians credit that "Battle of the Sexes," viewed by some 80 million Americans, as *the* event that triggered the tennis boom. Perhaps this Tribuno tournament could do the same for platform tennis.

During one of the matches Gene asked me what I thought about the future of paddle. At the time I was deeply involved in practically all aspects of the game. A line of paddles bore my signature. Dick Squires clothing ("Squirrel" line) was being marketed—even a playing glove (S.A.I.). Pro-Keds promoted a paddle sneaker that I endorsed, the Royal Edge. Later PUMA did the same. I was building "Squires Modular Courts" all over the country. Somehow I had been given the name "Mr. Platform Tennis," or, even sometimes (to my dismay), the "father of platform tennis." So my reply to Gene's question was, needless to say, upbeat. "Platform tennis is but a single serve away from becoming America's most popular athletic pastime."

It sounded good, but, alas, I was wrong.

In an attempt to bring the sport to the cities in 1976, I convinced Pro-Keds to sponsor a professional two-day tournament that was played on a temporary court erected in midtown Manhattan—on the plaza in front of Burlington House, 54th Street and the Avenue of the Americas. The teams played for $20,000 ... a lot of money in those days! With all the traffic that passed by each day, people looking out of their office windows from surrounding multi-storied skyscrapers, plus the hundreds or thousands of pedestrians that stopped by to ascertain "what was going on in that cage," there is no question that more spectators viewed those matches than all the other paddle contests combined since the birth of the sport. It must have been in the millions!

10

Of course, probably less than 1 percent knew what they were watching, but it was wonderful exposure for the traditional country club game.

Subsequently, in 1977, the Apple Platform Tennis Club opened up with six courts located on top of a nine-story apartment complex on East 24th Street. That same year an opportunistic editor, Bob Abrams, began publishing a slick magazine called <u>PADDLE WORLD.</u> In short order it folded, but not before I had some fun writing a column entitled "Playing the Wires with Dick Squires." (Perhaps I helped the publication to fold!)

So, too, did the pro tour. By the latter part of the '70s, Tribuno, Passport Scotch and Hertz had all come and gone as sponsors of pro play. Their board of directors must have questioned what their corporations were getting in return for endorsing this comparatively small, elitist game. With the departure of these companies the professional game came to an end in 1980.

By the Golden Jubilee year, 1978, it was conjectured that the total number of U.S. paddlers was nudging 400,000. (Again, however, it was unclear what the definition of a "player" was.) Canada had become interested. Courts were springing up in the Toronto area. Aluminum planking was rapidly replacing wooden boards as the standard for the decking. Metal courts were much more costly, but they were heatable and far less expensive to maintain.

While the winter circuit tournaments were, once again, being played by amateurs for silver mugs rather than dollars, enthusiasm was still running high in the 1980s. By 1988 the APTA showed a listing of more than100 tournaments on its yearly schedule, with competition for 12-year-olds on up to the 65-plus age category. It was estimated that 500 clubs in the U.S. now had paddle courts. And youngsters were beginning to feed into the game. More emphasis was placed on junior play. In 1989, at the National Junior Boys' and Girls' championships, 176 participants–including 15 doubles teams from Canada—competed for titles.

Before the demise of the pro tour the Men's President's Cup competition was established in 1978 in order to have an arena for the somewhat overlooked amateur paddler. For several years the pro circuit got all the limelight. For the next three seasons this two-day event was scheduled separately from the Pro National Championships. When the pro events died, the Cup matches became a one-day prelude to the Nationals.

The APTA divided the country into six regions and the top five teams competed for the "glory" of their sections. In 1982 the Women's President's Cup was inaugurated and by 1990 it, too, became a five-team rivalry. Part of the tradition excludes the top-ranked eight teams from the competition.

As this updated edition of HOW TO PLAY PLATFORM TENNIS goes to press in the fall of 1992, there is talk about a new pro circuit sponsored by Vittert, the platform tennis ball manufacturer. I hope it happens.

For a sport to be "for real," it has to have a pro tour and spectators that are willing to pay dollars to see the best players perform.

A professional tour featuring "the best players in the world" shows the uninitiated how well the sport can be played. It excites and encourages people to try the sport, to improve, to become as adroit, one day, as the pros.

12

The money on the tour will initially be minimal. It will attract, once again, however, some of the better, younger athletes to the sport as it did back in the middle to late 1970s. That will be good.

The "old guard" will protest again. Some of them will complain about the sport "being ruined" and the "wrong kind of people are playing it only because of the dollars." It's the classic argument that the "white beards" of the tennis world used for so many years. When they finally lost their pleas for continued amateurism and professional "open" tennis became a true reality in 1968, that once pure, pristine, elitist sport became a popular pastime worldwide.

Today more than 22 million Americans play tennis and over 180 countries around the globe have organized tennis associations. Could it happen to platform tennis? Probably not. But, as I did 20 years ago, dreaming is nice even though it seldom becomes a reality.

In an effort to find out how many platform tennis players there were in the U.S., the Racquet Sports Committee of the Sporting Goods Manufacturers Association commissioned American Sports Data to obtain an estimate. Their 1992 survey revealed that 478,000 Americans were playing the game – 100,000 regularly.

It is difficult to predict here in 1992 what the future holds for this great paddle and ball sport. I certainly have been wrong in past prognostications. I am convinced, however, even though it most likely will never be a sport for the masses, that platform tennis will continue its steady growth. Why? Because it is a super "product" and timely for the '90s.

I defy you to name another athletic pastime that offers so much for so many. It fills the bill for family togetherness activities, it's fun and exciting, and provides a good, healthy aerobic form of outdoor exercise during those frigid days and nights of winter. It is a good deal easier to learn than tennis (particularly if you play tennis), but is as difficult to master. That damnable single serve and those intimidating rebounds off the screens are constant challenges, even for the most skilled players.

But, trust me, once you start sensing some palpable improvement you will be "hooked" for life. When you wake up some Saturday morning in, say, January, look at the outdoor thermometer shivering in the teens, see the new-fallen snow on the ground, and the forecaster on the radio predicts "colder and flurries," you will rub your hands together with glee. It is "perfect paddle weather," and you are looking forward to your doubles game at 10 a.m. You are animated, because you know how great you are going to feel after playing three brisk sets. Your cheeks will be rosy, your cotton turtleneck shirt will quickly be soaked with perspiration, and, while tired, your body will be thriving from such a marvelous workout.

So even though not a single splinter is left of the Old Army Athletes' original court, we are truly indebted to those early pioneers of paddle in Scarsdale, N.Y. They not only invented a fantastic game, but they were willing to promote and share it with us.

Read on. Chances are real good that you, too, will become an addicted "paddle nut."

chapter 2
The serve

Author's Note: In the original printing of "HOW TO PLAY PLATFORM TENNIS," I did not cover the serve until Chapter 3. In retrospect, this was two chapters too late. Developing a reliable serve is an extremely important aspect of paddle. One of the game's unique (and frustrating) features is the fact that you only have a single serve. One fault means a lost point. There is no reprieve. Other racquet and paddle sports allow the luxury of a second serve if the first one is a fault. Not so in platform tennis.

The main difference between a "B" paddler and an "A" is the ability of the better player to hit a serve he or she has confidence in—no matter what the score happens to be.

The majority of mediocre players content themselves for years just (whew) pooping the ball into play. They don't practice improving their delivery to the point where it is an effective, offensive one. If you want to improve your overall game, start with the serve. When you arrive at the point where you have developed a spin serve you can hit and place in the opponent's court with confidence, you will have raised your skill level one or two notches. I promise.

D eveloping a *dependable* serve is perhaps even more important than ultimately developing an effective or offensive one. You are allowed just one serve, which makes American platform tennis unique in the world of racquet/paddle sports that employ overhand serves. Tennis, squash racquets, squash tennis, court tennis, hard racquets– all permit two serves. In addition, placing the ball in the proper service area is easier in those games.

It is not unusual for even the best tournament-toughened platform tennis players to "choke" on their serves during crucial games—sometimes to the point where two, three and, yes, even four consecutive balls fail to find their mark in the opponent's service box. Such a collapse can completely shatter the confidence of a player and have disastrous effects on the rest of his game–not to mention his partner's!

So, first and foremost, is the absolute necessity to develop a *consistent* serve with which you feel comfortable and confident. Some players have actually used a reliable *underhand* slice serve to be doubly certain the ball is put in play, but this is the last resort. Merely putting the ball into play is not good enough if you want to be an adept paddler.

The best serve is one that you control by applying spin to the ball. A flat serve, while easier to learn, just doesn't cut it in paddle. It's predictable and sits up too high. The opposition will kill it. Spin is applied by opening up, or laying back the paddle face slightly (toward the backhand grip). This facilitates your getting some "bite" on the ball, and bite is control.

Don't be concerned about the lack of speed at first. A hard-hit, clean "ace" in platform tennis is practically as rare as a no-hitter in baseball.

Even if you are a novice, you should start out with

a modified *spin* serve. Eventually you will be playing and practicing to develop an effective, offensive delivery that gives your opponents trouble. You will show little improvement, on the other hand, if you hit the ball with a flat paddle. The rest of your game may improve, but the lack of an effectual serve will retard your overall progress, unless you get off to a running start by developing a reliable, controlled spin serve.

Basically, the platform tennis serve is a shorter, more contained version of the classic tennis stroke. It is more restrained, however—rather like the *second* serve in tennis. After all, with only one serve it would be imprudent to just lean back and let it rip. Plus, if you hit the ball too hard (if you don't fault), the ball will rebound out from the back wires and the opponents can execute an offensive return.

The proper starting position is with the paddle and ball touching and out in front of you at approximately eye level. Your body should be positioned sideways to the net with your weight resting comfortably on the rear foot. The front foot should be placed one or two inches away from the baseline in order to prevent foot-faulting (stepping on or over the baseline prior to hitting the ball—a common malady with thousands of paddlers!). Your feet should be so aligned that if someone took a straight stick and placed it across the tips of your sneakers it would point precisely to that point on the court you are intending to place your serve.

Stand about three to four feet to the right or left of the center, so that your approach to the net behind your serve is on an angle. This position will help cut off the angle of your opponents' returns.

There are two theories regarding the first stage of the serving motion. One theory states you should

Proper position of feet for serving into left or deuce court. A ruler placed at tip of sneakers would point directly to where the server will place the ball.

Proper line-up of feet for serving into right or ad court. Server is also situated about three feet to the left of center.

merely pull your paddle directly back to the cocked position behind your head and then make your toss-up of the ball. The other theory, which I recommend, is that the paddle and the ball should be pulled down simultaneously by just dropping your hands. There is absolutely no work involved in this initial step. As a matter of fact, it helps to keep you relaxed and your service motion grooved. In addition, by employing this "sweeping" windup you are also building up a certain degree of momentum.

At a comfortable point just above the kneecaps the hand holding the paddle will almost automatically and effortlessly continue on back to a position approximately level with the right ear. The wrist is cocked and back. As you pull down on the paddle and ball, your body weight shifts from the back toward the front foot.

At the same time you make the all-important, precise toss-up. When you toss the ball up be sure to keep your head up. Some players make the mistake of throwing the ball up, then looking to the spot they plan to hit it. Golfers have to keep their heads down; platform tennis servers must keep their heads up!

Having most of your weight on the forward foot helps you apply a little pace on the ball. Also, by falling forward, you will gain a few extra valuable steps on your way to the net behind your serve. And, remember: *You must always go to net behind your serve.*

Reach up and strike the ball at the *apex* of the toss-up. At the moment of impact, your hitting arm should not be bent but fully extended. As a matter of fact, your entire body should be stretched out to its full height. This will help you place the ball in your opponent's court. Employing the "Continental" (toward the backhand) grip will help you "bite" or "cover" the ball with the paddle. Spin is applied by snapping your wrist forward and down at the instant of impact.

There are two types of spin serves you should attempt to develop. Both are hit with a semi-open paddle face and wristy motion.

The *twist* serve is usually employed when trying to place the ball to your opponent's *backhand.* To twist a serve, your paddle head should make contact with the ball at the top and slightly to the *left* side of the ball.

The ball is tossed slightly behind your head, so that your back has to arch

Gary's arm is fully extended as paddle contacts ball and weight is forward. The momentum is moving him toward the net.

19

Service Grip

prior to your impacting the ball. This imparts some top, as well as reverse, spin that causes the ball to bounce to the right or toward your opponent's backhand side.

It is well to add here that you cannot, and should not, expect to attain as much "bite" or spin on the ball using a wooden, laminated paddle as is possible with a strung tennis racquet. The smooth, sponge rubber ball cannot be "grabbed" by the even, solid paddle the way a strung racquet can truly bite the inflated, hollow tennis ball.

The side spin or "slice" serve is used most often when you want to put the ball wide to your adversary's forehand. The toss-up for this serve is usually thrown slightly off to the right of your normal toss-up. This will help you come across the ball, which, in turn, will give a wider angle of trajectory. By contacting the ball on the right side, you keep the ball spinning away from your opponent's forehand, or to the left, after it lands in his service court.

If the top of the ball is 12 o'clock, the twist is hit at approximately 11 o'clock and the slice at 3 o'clock.

The follow-through is just as important as the stance, windup, toss-up and impact. You must follow through *completely* to your left side in order to ensure everything you have put into the serve stays in. Not following through on the serve is the same as a boxer

The twist service

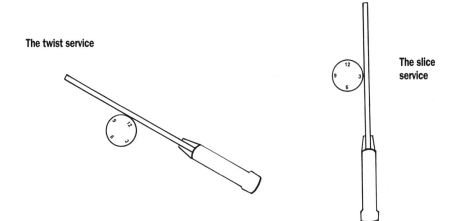

The slice service

winding up from the floor for a knockout punch, then ending up delivering a jab that travels no more than two inches. What an utter waste of motion and potential power! What a superfluous amount of excessive work and needless energy.

In addition, you are actually doing extra work if you fail to follow through to the left side. It takes effort to stop that heavy paddle from going all the way through naturally after making contact with the ball.

So, first and foremost, work on creating a serve that has some spin on it, and then develop the confidence that you can *place* the ball to specific target areas in the opposition's service boxes. If you uncover certain weaknesses, serve to them. Also, try to *move your opponent.* Do not allow him the luxury of planting his feet and walloping his return-of-serve right at you or your partner. Keep him off balance and guessing. Don't always serve to the same place. Prevent him from anticipating where you are going to hit the ball by serving to different spots.

The majority of serves, however, should be aimed at your opponent's weak side. It should not take too many serves for you to discover from which side he prefers to return the ball—forehand or backhand.

Occasionally a serve *right at* your opponent pays

SERVE[ABOVE]: Connie Jones serving from the "usual" position at the baseline.

SERVE [BELOW]: To direct serve toward "ad" court [backhand], she moves toward her alley.

22

Serving wide to forehand, Jones will come in at such an angle that she will be able to cover a variety of cross-court returns.

high dividends—as when a baseball pitcher "jams" the batter. Serving straight at the opponent also prevents him from getting off a wide-angled return.

A "cream puff" serve, while safe, will be a definite handicap when up against good players. If you want to be competitive, you must work on a spin serve. Then, as confidence comes, try to apply a little more pace so that the serve becomes an offensive *weapon* rather than just a way to start the point. Also, when practicing, hit most of the serves to the deuce (left-hand court) down the middle. When serving to the right-hand or ad court, aim toward the right corner of the service box. In other words, hit the ball toward your opponent's backhand, as that is usually the weaker stroke.

As mentioned previously, the limiting factor of having only one serve can be rather unsettling, especially during pivotal games in the din of competition. The single serve builds character. If you feel a "creeping tightness" coming over you, it will help immensely to pause, take a few deep breaths, and toe the baseline for a deliberate second or two prior to making the next serve. Even untying and retying a shoelace will help your composure.

When the match is about to start, be sure to take *at least* two practice serves into *both* the deuce and ad courts prior to serving "for real." Make sure the last practice serve goes in. If all your practice serves are faults, keep hitting until you get one in. Don't handicap yourself on your first "for real" serve by having to adjust in order to get the ball in play. Have a real "feel" for the ball on the paddle prior to actually starting to play.

Even some of the more skilled players have developed a bad habit when playing just for fun. When their turn comes to serve, they take a few practice serves and then say, "First one in." This is not only unfair to the receiver—since all pressure is now off the server—but it can cause problems when the server has to serve consistently under the pressure of "live" competition.

When practicing, therefore, it should be under simulated tournament conditions. Otherwise you will discover the tension and stress is much worse when you are involved in a tournament, and chances are you will have more of a tendency to clutch on those first few deliveries.

SERVICE RECAP:
- Game rules permit only *one* serve.
- First and foremost, *get the ball into play.*
- Secondly, develop a *controlled spin* (twist or side spin) serve with some pace on it. This only comes in time with practice. Don't change it when

competing in tournaments. Keep serving briskly *even if you are faulting a lot.* That is the only (painful) way you will groove an improved serve that you can hit consistently under pressure.

• Work on *placing* the ball and hitting it *deep* toward your adversary's backhand.

• Keep your opponents off balance by *moving* the served balls to various target areas.

• Try to serve to your opponent's *weakness.*

• You must *always* go to net behind your serve.

• Take a *minimum* of four practice serves and make sure the last one is good.

chapter 3
The ground strokes

*A*uthor's Note: There are a few good players who have developed sound, forceful backhands, but very few. Most of the top paddlers have offensive forehands as the dominant weapon in their arsenal of strokes. The relative smallness of the playing area, and the fact you have a partner covering half of the court, mean you can pretty much "hide" or run around your backhand. So, while it is important to execute a steady, sure backhand, you should concentrate on mastering a powerful, forceful and consistent forehand.

If you have played any tennis at all, you should have little trouble hitting platform tennis ground strokes. Just keep in mind that the court is approximately half the size of a tennis court; therefore, it is not necessary to hit long, flowing strokes. In addition, obtaining depth on your ground strokes (which a player strives for in tennis) is not only unnecessary, but undesirable, because of that great equalizer, the back screen. Also, your opponents are much nearer to you than in tennis, so there isn't as much time to execute long, smooth strokes.

So, while the fundamental forehand and backhand strokes are similar to tennis, by necessity your swing will be shorter, somewhat faster, and the ball will be hit with an abbreviated follow-through.

Of paramount importance is consistency and this

steadiness can only be realized by using controlled spin when hitting ground strokes.

1. Forehand: The Eastern tennis grip is the most widely used and accepted way of holding the paddle. Take the paddle into your hand, hold the hitting surface at right angles to the ground and merely shake hands with the grip. That is the proper grip.

The moment your opponent hits a shot in the direction of your forehand, start your paddle up and back immediately, but slowly. By beginning your backswing early, you preclude the necessity of making a last second wind-up and a fast "flick" stroke. All your ground strokes should be hit as smoothly and as effortlessly as possible. Attempt to time the backswing so that you are taking your paddle back at the same pace as the ball is traveling on its way toward you. This will help your timing and overall rhythm. From backswing to follow-through the movement of the paddle should be *continuous* and *fluid*.

Contact is made slightly farther back than on backhand. At moment of impact, the hitting arm is fully extended. Again, weight is moving forward into the shot.

It is important to turn sideways (when you have the time) and step forward as your paddle meets the ball. As with *all* the basic strokes, you should try to have your body *weight,* not merely your arm, behind your shots. Everything moving forward, or in the

28

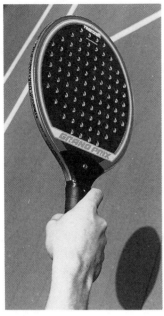
Forehand grip

direction of your shot, will help groove your stroke, and will also put far more "sting" or pace on the ball.

a) Topspin Forehand: As your paddle makes contact with the ball, roll your entire forearm slightly (toward the net), keeping the wrist locked. This causes the paddle to "cover" the ball, so to speak, and you have applied controlled topspin that will keep the ball low and in the court. In time and with practice, you will "feel" exactly how much spin is required to gain the desired control and pace and feel confident doing so.

Your follow-through should be out in front and in the direction of where you are trying to place the ball. Again, the paddle follow-through is not as pronounced or as long a stroke as in tennis. The follow-through should also be higher than the height of the net. If it is not, chances are the ball will go into the net and you have lost the point on an error.

b) Slice Forehand: On the sliced forehand, your paddle contacts the ball on the underside and

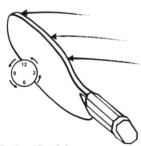
Forehand Top Spin

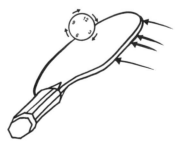
Forehand Slice

29

backspin (as against topspin) is thereby applied.

The slice forehand is usually employed as a defensive return—when you are chasing after a ball and do not have time to get set and really "whack it." A high-bouncing ball will also have to be hit with a slicing motion. The slice forehand can, however, also be used effectively as a change of pace in order to surprise your opponents with an unexpected bounce.

As mentioned earlier, the topspin forehand is hit with a "closed" paddle, whereas the slice forehand calls for an "open" paddle with the playing surface facing upward at about a 45-degree angle from the plane of the deck.

Unlike the topspin shot, you will use a snap of the wrist to impart the "cut" underspin to the ball. In reality, this stroke is hit quite similarly to the execution of a volley, with perhaps even more of an exaggerated "bite."

Slicing down on the ball also helps keep the ball low. Your opponents will have to hit up in order to make their returns.

2. Backhand: The backhand is also hit much like its counterpart in tennis, except, again, the swing is somewhat shorter. The grip, as in tennis, is a quarter of a turn (clockwise) of the paddle away from the forehand.

The instant the ball leaves the opponent's paddle and heads toward your backhand side (just as for all ground strokes), start taking your paddle *up and back.* This will prevent you from rushing your stroke. Many players are a fraction of a second late on their ground strokes due to a last-second backswing.

It is even more important on the backhand (than on the forehand) to *turn sideways* and to step into the ball

30

as you make your stroke. When you turn sideways, it is not a closed stance with the right foot crossed over toward the alley. It is a sideways stance with the right foot stepping *toward* the net. It is easier for most players to obtain much more power on the forehand; so in order to compensate and to add pace to your backhand, you must have your body weight moving into the ball as you hit.

You should make contact about three to six inches *in front* of your right toe (the forehand is hit approximately by your left heel). At the moment of impact the paddle head should be higher than the wrist. Keep your elbow tucked in next to your body; don't allow it to lead your paddle!

a) Topspin Backhand: On only rare occasions will you have enough time to hit a topspin backhand. The time to hit over the ball and to apply topspin to your backhand is when your opponent hits a soft shot that "sits up" and allows you to come in and "spank it."

On the backhand, ball is met out in front of right foot, weight forward. Follow-through is out front and higher than the net.

To hit the occasional topspin backhand, start with the paddle *below* the level of the ball, with your paddle face open. Then come over the ball with a roll of your wrist. The follow-through, again, is up and out over the height of the net.

b) Slice Backhand: Because of the lack of time, most of the more highly skilled players have developed a *hard* slice backhand shot, which provides speed and control and a ball with a low trajectory. There is a safety margin in this stroke and, if grooved low, you will compensate for the loss of power obtainable with a topspin backhand.

When executing this shot, the paddle head starts from a position higher than the ball (just the reverse of topspin), then sweeps through on an oblique angle, contacting the side and underneath part of the ball with the open face of the paddle. The cocked wrist, with the paddle still open, snaps through at or just above the height of the net, and, of course, in the direction you want to place the ball.

About 90 percent of your backhands should be hit with slice spin rather than topspin. After you have developed a good feel for a slice there is no reason why it cannot become an offensive shot.

GROUND STROKES RECAP:

• Forehand and backhand ground strokes are similar to tennis, with the exception of a *shorter, faster* swing and an *abbreviated follow-through.*

• *Consistency* and *steadiness*, rather than overwhelming power, are the keys to platform tennis ground strokes.

• Start your backswing *early*—the instant the ball leaves your opponent's paddle. This will keep you from rushing your swing.

• Whenever possible, turn *sideways* on all ground strokes, and *bend your knees* on low balls.
• Whenever possible, *step into* the ball.
• There are basically two types of ground strokes: *topspin* and *slice.*

Not only is it important to bend the knees on low bouncing balls, but sticking out his tongue also helps Tom Houlihan when making difficult returns.

Return of serve "ready position". Gary's paddle is up, his weight is forward, and he's on or inside the baseline to catch the served ball early.

34

chapter 4
The return of serve

*A*uthor's Note: If the serve is the most important stroke to master for a complete player, and I believe it is, the second most important is the return of serve. It is one of the few shots that offers you the opportunity to catch your opponent's serve early and really attack the ball. Unless your opponents have developed "big serves," you will have the time to hit a wide variety of returns that do damage and/or intimidate the serving team. Think positively and be aggressive when making your various returns. Although the serving team has the advantage of gaining the net position, good returns can diminish that advantage.*

The return of serve is perhaps the only stroke hit off your opponent's shot that frequently allows you the luxury of time to turn sideways, anchor your feet, wind up and smash the ball *offensively.* If the serve is not hit well, or properly placed, you will have the opportunity and time to step in and really crush the ball—often for a winner or a forced error. A hard-driven return of serve can be very intimidating to the incoming server.

About the most important elements to keep in mind when executing your return of serve are to catch the ball on the *rise* (right after it bounces), to *move into the ball* and to have your *body weight shifting forward* in the direction of your shot the moment your

paddle meets the ball. This will help you obtain greater pace to your return, and it also puts more pressure on the server as he races to net for his crucial return-of-serve volley. For a split second your opponent might think you are coming all the way in behind your return (blitzing) and, perhaps, he will be more prone to rush his volley. He might even take his eye off the ball to ascertain your intentions. There are many good reasons to catch the serve on the rise and be moving into the shot as you make your return.

Another fundamental aspect of this stroke is to start your backswing the instant the server strikes the ball. This will keep you from rushing your shot and from taking a last-second swipe at the ball.

You should position yourself as far in as your opponent's serve allows. The better his serve, the farther back (toward the baseline) you will be compelled to stand. The weaker the serve, the closer you can stand—even inside the baseline and closer to the net. Whenever possible, try to position yourself no farther back than just *inside* the baseline.

36

While you are waiting for your opponent to serve to you, assume a semi-crouched position, bent over slightly from the hips and leaning forward with your body facing the net. Since you can probably return more effectively off your forehand, position yourself toward the backhand side of the service box. Your feet should be spread comfortably, weight forward on the soles of your sneakers, the knees slightly flexed and never stiff, and your paddle pointing more or less in the direction of the net.

Hold the paddle's grip loosely. This will help you relax. The paddle head should be up rather than down and out in front of you in a position from which you can hit either a forehand or a rare backhand return at will. This is the "ready" position, and you will be prepared to move quickly in any direction once your opponent serves. Generally speaking, the waiting or ready stance in platform tennis is the typical athlete's stance— one that helps the hitter move rapidly and catlike in any direction.

The return of serve is the *second* most vital stroke; only the serve

Squirrel's eye view of Mike Gillespie receiving serve from ad court and making sure he gets the forehand he wants.

takes priority. As with other platform tennis shots, the key is *consistency*. No matter what shot you attempt, do whatever is necessary to make certain the ball clears the net. It is always better to hit out (long) of court on your errors than into the net. First and foremost, therefore, is to *return* the return of serve! Force your opponents to make a volley. Don't give away points by hitting the net.

While you are returning, you should concentrate solely on watching the ball come off your opponent's paddle. Your eyes, your mind, and your total concentration should be zeroed in on that ball and where you plan to hit it. If the serve pulls you wide, or comes right at you, you will not have time to think about what to do with the ball. Your movement and return will have to be accomplished instinctively. This instinct can be developed with play and practice.

When making the return of serve, the same axiom for all paddle strokes holds true; *mix up* your shots as much as possible.

Bare–legged Gillespie is ready for anything as he awaits serve with his backside literally pressed against the screen.

Unless you discover an obvious defensive or offensive weakness in your opponent's play (for example, the man at net is afraid of a ball aimed right at him, or the serve is very weak, which provides you the opportunity to make a "kill" practically every time), try to make a *different* return every time. Keep your opponents off-balance, wary and worried. Do not ever let them know what or where your next return will be.

The best and most logical return of serve is hit fairly *hard* and *low,* straight down the *middle.* The net man on the other side of the court will not "poach" (cross over and cut your ball off with a volley), and the incoming server will have to "dig" in order to make an effective return volley. Keep in mind the age-old center theory: "The safest and most effective place to hit the ball when the competition has control of the net position is down the middle between them." This is your "bread and butter," high-percentage return.

An effective variation on the return of serve is the *dink.* This is a very short, soft, sharply angled crosscourt shot that just barely clears the top of the net. It will draw your opponent (the incoming server) wide and away from the center. If he is ambling in— rather than charging—you might well catch him in an awkward position where he is compelled to half volley or make a weak volley that "sits up." The dink also draws him away from protecting the middle, and your next return should be down the middle. Keep 'em guessing!

Another option is a hard hit shot aimed right at the opposing net man. If he is at all jittery about being up at the net, a well-aimed forehand lashed right at him or down his alley (hit early in the match) will do wonders to further undermine his confidence. This occasional shot will also "keep him honest." He will not be too apt to poach, as you have made him aware you can hit "down the line" as well as cross court.

A lob return placed deftly over the head of the opposing net man is another variation of the return of serve that will keep the serving team off-balance and edgy. If the server comes to net like a runaway locomotive, try lobbing over his head a few times.

It is important to analyze your opponents' serves, where they position themselves, as well as how they advance to the net. Do they move the serve around to different spots in your service box? Can they place it to your backhand, or do they invariably serve to your forehand? Do they come to net slowly or like a charging rhino? Does the net man attempt to move out and volley your cross-court returns, or is he fairly content to stay on his side of the court? How close does the net man stand to the net? Is he vulnerable for a lob or a brisk forehand aimed at his chest? In other words, study your rivals carefully early on in the match and vary your returns accordingly.

Above all, remember that this particular stroke is called the *return* of serve. Consistency and variation will pay far more dividends than successfully making one in five sensational, hard-hit shots down the net man's alley.

RETURN OF SERVE RECAP:
   • This is one of the few shots in platform tennis that affords you the *time* to wind up and hit a powerful, *offensive* shot. Take advantage of these rare occasions.
   • Stand in as *close to the service line* as the opponents' serves permit, meet the ball *on the rise* and move forward as you impact the ball.

40

- *Consistency* is the key when making this shot.
- *Mix up* your returns as much as possible. Keep your rivals guessing and on edge.
- An array of options:
   a) Low and down the middle.
   b) Hard right at the opposing net man.
   c) Lob over opposing net man's head, or the incoming server's.
   d) A wide-angled, soft and low "dink."

chapter 5
Blitzing

*A**uthor's Note: Generally speaking, today's paddler is younger and, therefore, more daring and aggressive than those who competed in my day. They are also, arguably, better and fitter athletes. Whenever they sense an opening, they go for it.*

If the opponents have weak serves, it will afford you the opportunity to attack the ball, not merely return it. Current players often launch an attack off their return of serve and make (or try to make) frequent forays toward the net behind their shots. This is called "blitzing." When I was competing regularly back in the 1960s, such a tactic was considered reckless and was seldom done.

Even today, such a relatively bold tactic is reserved for better players who have mastered a variety of returns of serve and have developed the confidence so that blitzing is a high-percentage, offensive strategy. They also have a fleet-of-foot partner who stays back in case their solo charge toward the net has to be aborted!

"B**litzing," or going to net behind a good, low return of serve, is a tactic that, if done well, will win you many quick points. Unlike tennis, where it is important for a doubles team to come to the net or stay back at the baseline together, in platform tennis your *partner* should *stay back* while you blitz in order to protect you in case your return sits up and allows your opponents to volley the ball at

43

Jones returns serve cross court low and hard.

She follows her return in (blitzes) while partner covers for her by staying behind at baseline.

or past you.

This is probably the only instance in any doubles racquet sport where the so-called "I formation" (your partner directly behind you) can pay off.

When you start in behind your return, your partner should leave his side of the court and move toward the middle of the baseline in order to protect the entire backcourt. From this position he will be

44

able to cover the court better if a ball is hit by or through you.

Jones returns and Squires "surprises" opponents by blitzing and picking off volleyed return. Jones covers Squires by staying back in case foray fails.

Obviously, you will be compelled to return to the baseline as quickly as possible if your "mission" fails because of an ineffective return. Your partner would be smart (depending upon how much trouble you are in) to lob, thus giving you more time to retreat to the baseline.

On the other hand, if your return is a good one, low and hard, then your opponent will be forced to volley up. By advancing in behind your shot you will be in excellent position to volley the ball for a winner.

The best place to volley is between the opposing players or right at them. Be sure not to hit the volley too hard as the opposition will undoubtedly be retreating, and ideally, you do not want the ball to come off the back screen.

BLITZING RECAP:

•*Move in* toward the net behind a hard, low return of serve.

•Your partner *stays back,* moves toward the center of the baseline and covers the entire back court, thereby offering you protection.

•The logical place for a putaway volley is *between* or *right at your opponents,* but not too hard hit.

chapter 6
Screen play

Author's Note: The screens, and being able to use them, represent the essence of the sport of platform tennis. They, along with the single serve and small court, are the intriguing equalizers. They are the reasons why power is secondary, why placement, patience and playing the percentages are virtues that reap rewards.

Watch the top players during a typical, extended point. It is likely the ball will traverse the net 30 to 40 times before the rally ends. Why? Because, at this advanced level of play, it is difficult for anyone to hit an outright winner.

The serving team has control of the net, but the receiving team has that "third partner" to help them; i.e., the side and back screens. That's right. They are an _ally_, not an adversary.

There is a beautiful, relaxed rhythm to "playing the wires" once you become proficient at it. The better players appear loose, almost nonchalant, when executing their lobbed (usually) returns. They possess the confidence that they will be able to return _anything_ their opponents hit at them.

I have often been asked how I can make screen play look so easy and effortless. The reply is always the same—practice and patience.

47

laying the ball off the wires—side and back screens—is probably the most difficult part of platform tennis to learn and eventually to master. But it is a vital and essential ingredient of the game if you aspire to become a top player and competitor.

If you have played any squash or four-wall handball/racquetball, you should understand the angles and paddle work required for platform tennis far more readily than the individual who has played neither.

The best and actually only way to learn the "wire work" is practice, practice and more practice. There is just no substitute and no easy way. No book has been written that can tell you precisely where to stand to retrieve a ball coming off the screens. There are too many angles and variables.

If the screens are true and tight (and each court seems to vary somewhat), a ball angled into the screen will come off at the same angle. This is a fundamental law of geometry. Another variable, besides the tension of the wires, is, of course, the speed at which the ball is hit into the screen.

Back Screen: Most beginners have trouble with the ball coming directly off the the back screen primarily for one reason. They will wait until the ball is practically on top of them before starting their backswing. They wind up and swing their paddle at the last possible instant as the ball rebounds. Wrong!

There should be a smoothness to screen play, and in order to feel relaxed and comfortable in returning balls off the wires it is absolutely essential that you make your backswing as the *ball goes by you* on its way to the rear screen. In so doing, your paddle is *behind the ball* and ready to make a fluid, effortless

48

return as the ball rebounds out. This early backswing avoids a last-second "flick" (frequently a "whiff"), or an uncontrolled return.

Another basic fundamental of all screen play is to *position your feet and body,* whenever time permits, *behind the ball* prior to hitting. It is always better to go too far into the screen and then follow the ball out, rather than to be too far in front of it to obtain the leverage or strength to return the ball. Don't wait for the ball to come out to you. Go in after it!

The vast majority of your returns off the back (as well as side/back) screens should be *lobs.* Your opponents are both up at net and you and your partner are in the backcourt on the defense. While a ball may occasionally come out high and far enough for you to make an offensive return, the best shot will invariably be a safe lob.

Most beginners or mediocre players do not *use* the back screen enough. They somehow feel it exists only as a last resort, a crutch, when all else has failed, or when their opponents have laced a ball by them. This is a completely erroneous concept, mainly brought on by fear of screen play through inexperience. They do not understand it is very possible to play the ball off the back screen to an *advantage.* A lack of confidence often causes them to cut the ball off before it can reach the back screen. Again, a hurried, off-balance stroke can often cause needless errors and lost points. *Wait!* You really have a lot more time than you think, and the back screen is providing it. The *screens are your friends* and helpful allies.

Most novices have little or no concept of how to play balls off the back wire. While learning, they rarely hit balls hard or deep enough when they play against each other to bring on many screen shots.

When these beginners enter tournaments and their opponents slam overheads past them, they are apt to freeze and just automatically say, "Nice shot." Meanwhile, the ball has rebounded off the back wire and could easily have been returned if they had had some idea of how to hit a screen shot.

How often have you seen both men and women make a hurried, frantic half-volley of a deep, hard shot right at the baseline, and subsequently dump the ball into the net? If they had only stepped aside, allowed the ball to go into the back screen (which, in turn, allows them more time!) and taken it as it came back, their percentage of needless errors would be drastically reduced.

The better female players often do not have superior ground strokes or net games than many other women. They have, however, through the years of playing mixed doubles, learned to be relaxed, and to return their opposition's shots off the screen in a steady and effective manner. More than anything else, their knowledge of the wires sets them a notch above. Screen play does not intimidate them. As a matter of fact, they like being challenged.

If the particular foursome you frequently play in does not hit the ball with enough pace to require screen play, you and your partner can practice alone. Have her (or him) stand across (and near) the net. This position in the forecourt will make it easier for her to hit the ball deep and into the back screen. Keep lobbing to her so that she can hit overheads with some pace and high into the back screen for you to retrieve. You will be absolutely amazed how a 15-minute workout like this once or twice a week will improve your screen play and give you poise and confidence. It is an integral part of the sport, especially if you aspire to compete in top-flight doubles tournaments eventually.

Once you have become proficient and sure of your screen play, there is no reason why you cannot make an occasional *offensive* shot off the back screen if your opponents hit a ball that comes out high and far enough.

With experience you will quickly learn when the "right shot" occurs; that is, a ball that rebounds off the wires and affords you the time, opening and opportunity to drive it low and hard, either right at or between your startled opponents.

If you see that your offensive shot off the screen has caught the adversaries off-balance, it pays to follow your return in toward the net. Frequently, the element of surprise, plus the effect of your shot, will cause your opponents to make a weak return and, chances are, you can volley the "sitter" away for a winner.

Most players return screen shots from the ad court off the backhand.

Side Screen: A ball that lands deep in your court and travels first into the side screen and then the back screen is somewhat more difficult to return than one that goes directly into the back screen.

Almost all *forehand side* of the court players will *back up* on a ball that travels from the

side to the back screen and return it off their forehands.

Many players on the *backhand side* of the court, however, do not necessarily back up and return off their backhands. Some of them take it on their forehand by turning with the ball, pivoting their bodies and following the ball's flight with their eyes. You can experiment with both methods as you are learning and decide for yourself which approach is best for you. Whichever one you eventually opt for, never get yourself in the awkward position of returning the ball when your back is to the net.

It is merely a matter of playing and practicing in order to learn the angles, and how the speed of your opponent's shots affect these angles. The *only* answer to feeling comfortable on the side-back screen shots is to practice and *keep practicing.* This is the only way to learn these angles, where the ball is going to end up and where you should position yourself to make effortless (and even offensive) returns.

A return hit softly by the opposition had better be picked off as it rebounds off the side wire *before* it goes into the back screen, or it might well die before you can return it. A hard-hit shot will, on the other hand, rebound far out into the court, and you will have to hustle forward to be in the right spot to return it.

A ball that goes into the corner where the back and side screens meet and rebounds parallel to the side wire (a "hugger") is best "scooped off" rather than "picked off." That is to say, run the edge of your paddle along the wire surface, with the hitting area of the paddle at right angles to the screen. With a loose wrist, try to "wipe" or "scrape" the clinging ball off the screen and over to your opponent's side of the net.

52

Your chances of making a satisfactory return by employing this "safer" technique of scooping a side wire hugger are far better than trying to pick the ball off–which often results in an error.

On the side-back screen shots, as with *all* platform tennis strokes, it is vital to get your paddle back as quickly as you can. Even as you are chasing after the ball

Jay Packer is attempting to scrape or wipe the ball off this side screen "hugger" rather than trying to pick it off.

and following it as it rebounds off the screens, pull your paddle back and have it in a ready, cocked position prior to hitting. A last-second windup will invariably result in a miss or an error.

As with straight in and out back-wire shots, when the right opportunity presents itself along the side screen, there is no reason why you must continue to lob or feel you have to remain on the defensive. If one of your opponent's returns comes out far and high enough, you can certainly try to "pop it" hard and make a powerful, offensive shot. Practice and experience will tell you when this opportunity arrives.

Another basic rule for ground strokes holds true for screen shots as well; that is, whenever possible, try to get *down* to the level of the ball. On many occasions when hitting the side-back wire returns you will be retrieving a ball that is slowly dying (nearing

53

Jones is returning a low shot off the back screen. Her body is behind the ball and by bending her knees, she is down to the level of the ball. The paddle face is open, indicating a lobbed return.

the playing deck). You will have to "dig" for it. Your chances for success will be greatly enhanced if you bend *your knees* and hit from a crouched position.

SCREEN PLAY RECAP:

•Screen play is the most *difficult* part of platform tennis to learn, and there is absolutely no substitute for *practice* if you wish to be a proficient wire player.

•Take your backswing as the *ball goes by you* and travels into the screens. Your paddle must be behind the ball as it rebounds.

•Position your feet and body *behind* the ball prior to hitting. Do not wait for the ball to come out to you. *Go in after it!*

•Use the screens to an *advantage. Wait!* You have far more time than you think.

•Somewhere between 80 and 90 percent of the balls you return off the screens will (and should) be *lobs.*

•An *offensive* shot can, however, be made off the

screens once you master the rhythm, angles and timing, and are feeling comfortable returning screen shots.

• Bend your knees and "dig" for low, slow, dying balls.

• Think of the screens as your *friends.* They are not electrified. Use them the way an adroit boxer uses the ring ropes.

• Once you get the rhythm of playing the wires, you are well on your way to becoming a complete and confident paddle player. You will also enjoy the sport a good deal more.

chapter 7
The volley

Author's Note: It is essential to develop a good firm volley since the team that can control and dominate the net position will usually win the match. Hitting the volleys with a slight "cut" will make the ball skid somewhat on the playing surface or die on the screens. The cut is applied with a slight downward snap of the wrist as you make contact with a low, weak return.

The majority of your volleys, however, will be a block made with a rather flat paddle face and an extra firm wrist.

The forehand or backhand volley in platform tennis is hit the same way as in practically all racquet games. The main difference, again, is that the back screen precludes, for the most part, the opportunity to "spank" a hard-hit drive volley past your opponents and away for a clean, outright winner. The back screen means your adversaries always have a (second) chance to retrieve anything, even when the ball has passed them and appears to be "ungettable."

Basically, the volley is hit with a slightly downward "jab" or block, with your wrist cocked, the paddle head up and slightly open. Tilt back the paddle face about 15 to 20 degrees from the 90-degree (perpendicular) plane employed for ground strokes.

The backspin automatically applied will enable you to take some speed off the oncoming ball.

When you become accustomed to volleying with subtle underspin, you will more easily execute an effective drop volley (see Chapter 9) from the identical starting position.

(The drop volley can be a very potent weapon in your bag of paddle shots, especially in the over-50 group.)

No windup or backswing is necessary when volleying. Of all the basic strokes, the paddle should be gripped as *tightly* as possible on the volley to make absolutely certain it does not budge or get shoved

backward upon impact with the ball. Squeeze your
paddle handle prior to meeting the ball when
volleying. A slight bit of wrist action is employed on
the volley, but in a regimented and firm manner.

Also, try to consciously reach out *in front* to meet
the ball. Whenever possible avoid allowing the ball to
come in too close to your body.

Your *short,* abbreviated follow-through should be
out and *down* and in the direction of where you want
the ball to go. The follow-through of the paddle head
should be pointing right at the top of the net. The
volley is more of a *punch* than a flowing stroke.
Through practice, you will ultimately learn how hard

and how deep, or how short and how softly, you should hit the ball in order to place it in a difficult or strategic spot on the opponents' side of the court.

Remember: You need not always be going for a winner in the back corners. An occasional volley aimed straight down the *middle* of your rivals'

backcourt, one that doesn't come out too far, is also an effective shot. This is especially true when you are up against a right-handed and left-handed team. In that case, your opponents will usually have two backhands down the center.

Unless a team has played together for a long time, there is often a moment of hesitation and

Who takes volleys down the middle?

Rule of thumb: the player who can get to the ball first.

indecision as to who will cover and take shots down the middle.

Once again, be sure to bend your knees for the low balls. On low balls the paddle, obviously, will have to be more open, or back farther to assure that the volleyed ball will clear the net.

An inexperienced player will usually have less of a problem hitting a forehand volley properly, but can run into difficulties on the backhand side. When

60

attempting to apply backspin to backhand volleys utilizing the required downward slicing motion, he is likely to make the mistake of raising his elbow upward. Lifting the elbow does help put backspin on the ball, but it also causes one to hit too far on the underside of the ball. The result is frequently a ball popped straight up rather than the crisp, low "skidder" intended and desired.

While executing a backhand volley, *keep your elbow down.* It will help you hit the ball on the backside rather than the underside. Two exercises are recommended for overcoming this common ailment, and each is practiced best when someone merely *throws* a ball right at your paddle while you are at net. In this manner you need not be concerned with form and can concentrate solely on the position of your elbow.

Backhand volley: Paddle head is up and slightly open. Jay Packer is sideways with weight on foot closest to net. Elbow is down.

In one drill, use your left hand to keep your hitting elbow down and next to your body. In the other drill, press a ball against your body, using your right elbow, while actually hitting the backhand volley. Either exercise will enable you to acquire the feel of the proper elbow position while making a backhand volley.

Preferably (and, again, there frequently is not enough time) try to get your body out of the way

61

by turning *sideways* to the net prior to hitting volleys. Also, attempt to lunge forward, your body weight moving into the ball. Do not back up as you are volleying. Leaning back on your heels will cause inconsistent and erratic shots on *all* your paddle strokes.

While up at net when your partner is serving, your paddle head should be up (slightly higher than the top of the net), out in front and somewhat toward the backhand side. Cradle the paddle loosely in your left hand, and from this position you are ready to move in

Classic up-at-net "ready position."

any direction with one motion. Your feet should be comfortably apart, with your weight forward on the toes. Flex your knees and bend over slightly from the waist. Your stance should be positioned approximately three feet from the net. This is the "ready position." By having your paddle both up and forward, you are prepared to volley practically any ball you can reach with the minimum amount of effort. About two-thirds of the volleys you make will be those right at you or toward the backhand side.

While at the net it is perfectly good sportsmanship to feign "poaching" (or moving across the court, parallel to the net) after your partner has served and is on his way to the net to join you. Such movements will concern and worry your opponents. They'll anticipate you are going across to cut off, or volley, their cross-court return of serve. They may, therefore, conceivably hit too wide on the cross-court return in an effort to place it beyond the reach of the poacher.

Classic backhand volley–out front, weight forward, body sideways, arm extended.

Or they might attempt to "keep you honest" and aim the return down your alley. If you were only faking the poach you will already be in the proper position to make an easy volley, as well as allow your partner more time to take an offensive position at the net.

Finally, by being active and animated at net, you will be

breaking your opponents' concentration and confidence in their returns of serves. They will be attempting to outguess you, to anticipate whether or not you are going to move across, and they should really be putting their efforts solely into hitting the ball back. You will help win many serves for your partner by employing this moving-about tactic.

VOLLEY RECAP:
•Paddle volleys are similar to tennis volleys. Basically, they are downward *jabs* with the *paddle head up* and slightly open.

•Hold the paddle *tightly, no wind-up* is necessary, and reach *out* in *front* to volley. Practically *no backswing* is necessary.

•Keep your elbow *down.*

•Volley *deep* toward your opponents' baseline and *not* too *hard.* Aim most *frequently* for the corners and *occasionally* down the middle.

•*Bend your knees* and *open* the paddle face (tilt back) on low returns.

•When your partner is serving, *poach occasionally* or *feign* poaching to keep the opposition honest and edgy.

Many time national champion Rich Maier's version of a running forehand volley–extending forward to make contact with the ball.

chapter 8
Return-of-serve volley

A uthor's Note: You <u>must</u> advance to the net behind your serve; therefore, (a) you must develop an effective delivery and, (b) you must develop a consistent return-of-serve volley. People who have just taken up the sport (and have not read HOW TO PLAY PLATFORM TENNIS), will invariably stay back at the baseline after serving. The opposing team merely poops the ball back and also stays back. Neither strategy makes much sense, unless you enjoy baseline patty cake!

In any match involving skilled, knowledgeable players, it is basically a struggle for each team to capture the dominant position—up at the net. That goal is what is behind practically every shot. Control of the net will give you control of the match.

There is nothing spectacular about the return-of-serve volley. It is an interim shot. It is merely a step in your relentless quest to join your partner up at net.

U nlike tennis, the platform tennis player does not have the option of going or not going in toward the net behind the serve. He must follow his serve in. There is no such formation in paddle as one partner up at net and one partner back (except when blitzing). Either you are *both* up at net or *both* back at the baseline if you are to be an effective team.

It is important to move in as *far* as you can behind

your serve before making that first volley. The ideal
court position for volleying your opponents' return-of-
serve is *inside* (toward the net) your own service line.
If you come in fast enough, you should advance at
least to this desired position. It means, of course, you
cannot make your approach casual. You really have to
charge the net in order to be in the proper position to
make that first critical volley.

Jones makes return-of-serve volley just inside service line...

Come to net as far as you can, but try to be
anchored, with your feet planted firmly on the deck, at
the moment you execute that first volley. If you are still
moving at the time the ball strikes your paddle, the
chances are good that the ball will sail out of court
because of the momentum imparted from your
forward movement.

The return-of-serve volley is one of the more
difficult shots in the game of platform tennis. Why?
Because unless you have executed a near perfect serve,
the return of serve, as mentioned earlier, is one of the
few strokes your opponents can really attack. If your
serve "hangs fat," either you or your poor defenseless
partner at net might well end up "eating" the ball—or,
at best, be forced to make a weak, "pushy" defensive

66

volley.

The correct spot for you to aim that first volley is *deep* into your opponents' backcourt, preferably toward the *rear corners* to keep them both back and away from the net. Or hit it toward the weaker player. It is practically impossible to hit a clean winner off a return-of-serve volley, even when your opponents' return is high and ineffective.

...then moves further in closer to net as rally continues. The team is now a "wall."

Remember, both your opponents are in the backcourt. The prime purpose of this volley, therefore, is to provide the opportunity and the time for you to assume the net position. This position is approximately the same distance away from the net as your partner, both of you thereby forming an offensive, protective and impenetrable wall. The No. 1 rule of winning platform tennis is: "The team that controls the net the majority of time will invariably win."

RETURN-OF-SERVE VOLLEY RECAP
•Move in as *close* to the *net* as you possibly can behind your serve in order to volley that first return.

•Be *anchored* (stationary) at the moment you impact the ball.

• Volley *deep* in your opponents' court—preferably toward the *rear corners.*

• *Rarely* go for a *winner.* The return-of-serve volley is essentially hit to provide you ultimately with better positioning at net.

chapter 9
The drop volley

*A*uthor's Note: The drop volley is the most subtle *of all paddle strokes and, unless you are right on top of the net, it is a <u>low</u>-percentage shot. In tennis, the drop shot can be especially effective because of the much larger court. Also, a strung racquet provides more touch or feel than the solid surface of a platform tennis paddle.*

A drop volley, however, does round out your arsenal of paddle weaponry and makes you more of a complete player. It can also make you a feared adversary, particularly in the over-50 competition!

Only a few of the top-ranking platform tennis players today employ a drop volley effectively. For those who lack a real "touch" or "feel" of the ball on the paddle head, it is an extremely difficult shot to hit with any degree of consistency. And if you do not hit it perfectly, you will end up in serious trouble. You and your partner will be at net with your opponents charging in to make an easy putaway, because your drop volley "dropped" too high or too deep (sat up) in your rivals' court, and there you are standing at net an easy target for a lost point. You have, so to speak, "baited your own hook."

A drop volley is hit the same as a regular net volley, except you should make every effort to "hold" your stroke (hide your intentions) as long as possible. The stroke itself is actually performed with a very *short, deft* touch of the paddle to the ball.

Your chances of success are greatly enhanced if you are right on *top* of the net rather than back in the usual correct volleying position (approximately three feet back from the net).

The basic idea behind hitting a drop volley is to deftly touch the ball with a short, chopping undercut motion, allowing it to barely clear the net, drop straight down and die. The well-executed drop volley will bounce on the other side no farther than three to four inches from the net. Even if your opponents have anticipated your intentions and can scamper up to the ball, retrieval is almost impossible because of the ball's immediate proximity to the net.

The follow-through is not quite the same on the drop volley as with the regular volley. When the ball makes contact with your paddle you should just barely *touch* it, then quickly withdraw the paddle rather than following through in the direction of the net. The drop volley is the ultimate in "touch."

The face of the paddle should be even more open than on your usual volleys because, ideally, you want to apply backspin to the ball. By imparting backspin, when the ball lands on the opponents' side of the court it will rebound back toward the net—making a return even more difficult.

Depending upon where your opponents are, either a straight drop right in front of you or a sharply angled cross-court drop volley aimed at the side screen can be equally effective.

Remember also, as with all your volleying shots, to be sure to plant your feet and have your paddle up and out in front of you after execution in anticipation of

Maier is executing a deft, cross-court angled drop volley. See how wide open the face of his paddle is. This assures the ball will land close to the net on the opponents' side.

possible retrieval by your opponents. Do not assume any of your shots are automatic winners. No matter how well you think you have hit the ball, expect your opponents to get to it. That way you are always prepared.

DROP VOLLEY RECAP:

• The drop volley is probably the most difficult shot to hit effectively and consistently.

• You must be right *on top of the net* to enhance your chances.

• *Barely touch* the ball and aim just to clear the net. Attempt to *apply backspin* with an open paddle.

• *Be prepared* for your opponents to retrieve the ball.

71

chapter 10
The half volley

A uthor's Note: *The half volley is a defensive shot that you should not become too proficient in hitting. If you have developed a steady, reliable half volley, it's a sure sign that you have either become slow-footed or you are frequently in the wrong court position.*

Back in the early '60s there was a marvelous player by the name of Zan Carver. This three-time national champion was renowned for his skill in half volleying. The truth of the matter was he was just plain lazy!

T he half volley is another basic stroke that cannot be taught too readily. Possessing fast reflexes is helpful, but there are some fundamentals to keep in mind that can help your half volleying.

A half volley is essentially a shot that has to be made when you are in trouble. The opposition has hit the ball right at your feet, and you have been caught in the embarrassing position (usually *out of position*) where you can neither volley nor get back in time to hit a ground stroke. The half volley is usually hit when you have been trapped somewhere around the service line or in "no-man's-land" between the service and baselines.

Because you are in trouble, you should immediately forget everything except *keeping your eye on the ball*. This will help you coordinate your paddle so that you will at least have a chance to block the shot

73

back. The half volley is a reprieve.

Another important precept when half volleying is to get your paddle *back* and *down* low enough to meet the ball just as it starts to rise off the playing deck. This means you should have your knees flexed and your entire body, from the waist up, should be bent.

You will hardly

have any time to take a backswing. Hit through smoothly, but with *far less* follow-through than employed with your *offensive volley.* Keep the paddle face *open* and your wrist locked in order to allow the ball a fair chance of clearing the net. The rest is timing, playing and practicing, and a little bit of luck.

HALF VOLLEY RECAP:

• *Watch* the ball *closely.*

• Catch low balls *on the rise, bend your knees* and have your paddle face *open.*

• The half volley is primarily a *defensive* shot hit when you are out of position. Don't get too good at hitting it.

• On this one the paddle does most of the work.

chapter 11
The lob

*A*uthor's Note: I cannot believe I did not mention the occasionally hit <u>very</u> <u>high</u> lob when covering this stroke 23 wonderful years ago.

While I am still convinced deep lobs are more effective than high ones, a very high lob can almost be put in the category of an offensive shot.

A lob hit 25 to 35 feet straight up in the air is an extremely hard shot for the opponents to time. The ball is dropping down at them from a great height, occasionally out of the sun or from above the illumination of the night lights, and to time an overhead perfectly under such conditions is no easy task.

The high lob not only can produce a mis-hit or error from your rivals, it can often buy you a good deal of much needed time if either you or your partner are suddenly caught badly out of position and there is a definite need to regroup.

*T*he lob is probably the most *frequently* employed stroke in the game of platform tennis. The key to hitting a *good* lob is to obtain as much *depth* as you can. Whether you hit the lob from a shot rebounding off the platform deck or the screens try, whenever possible, to lob deep. Height is important, but secondary to length.

Generally speaking, there are four occasions when you must or should lob:

1. For defensive reasons, when you are in serious trouble and have no recourse but to lob in order to stay in the point.

2. An unexpected change of pace.

3. When your opponents are hovering too close to the net.

4. For tactical reasons. For example, your opponents do not know how to put a lob away, or the sun might be directly in their eyes, etc.

The majority of lobs are hit as defensive shots; that is, when your opposition is at the net and has placed a ball that forces you out of position. As you can see from the many occasions cited that call for lobbing, there are actually two different types of lobs—the defensive one and the offensive one.

The well-hit *offensive* lob is placed rather low, so that its arc (flight of the ball) *just clears* your opponent's outstretched paddle. Needless to say, this shot takes a great deal of practice, but it is an integral part of your repertoire of strokes.

To become an effective lobber, it is, once again, essential to get your paddle back as quickly as possible. In other words, be prepared well in advance, which will help you disguise your shot and intentions. In addition, and to realize the best results, it is best to "hold" your shot and hide what you plan to do until the last second. By doing so, the opposing team will tend to be leaning forward in anticipation of a hard return, which will aid your efforts to drop the ball over their heads and beyond their reach. If hit correctly there is little chance of retrieval off the back screen. Most lobs are expected (when you are in trouble), but the unexpected lob can be an offensive gem. The element of surprise—when the competition is anticipating a hard-hit, low passing shot and you lob instead—is a great offensive tactic and a source of great personal satisfaction. So get your paddle back quickly and your feet in the proper position as though ready to drill a hard passing shot; a lob at this moment will be a most effective stroke.

Needless to say, if your lob successfully clears your opponents' paddles and they are forced to relinquish the net, be sure you and your partner take advantage of your good shot by racing to the net. Their normal return, if your ball does not die on the back wire, will probably also be a lob.

Keep in mind that the lob is a *full* stroke and not a short, quick stroke. You must follow through. The

backswing is the same as for your ground strokes, which, again, will disguise your lob. A quarterback in football employs the same windup for a short, "over the middle" pass as he does for a 60-yard "bomb"–only the follow-through varies. In platform tennis the follow-through, for a lob, is somewhat more elevated than on a ground stroke; but

Effective lobbing calls for an open paddle face and a high follow-through.

don't think of hitting only up. Consciously think of hitting the ball *out* and *up*.

Attempt to place the lob toward the *backhand* side

of your opponents. This will cause them to hit overheads from an off-balance, awkward position, and often will result in a poorly hit return or, better, a forced error.

Finally, a lob down the *center* frequently brings on confusion between the team members on the other side of the net, especially if they have not played together for any length of time. Each one will think the other is going to take it.

Nationally ranked Sarah Krieger's lobbing finish is both up and out.

LOB RECAP:

• Probably the most *frequently* employed stroke in the game.

• There are two types of lobs: *defensive* and *offensive.*

78

- On offensive lobs, *hold* your shot as long as you can.
- Get the paddle back *quickly*—as suggested for *all* paddle shots.
- Follow through both *up* and *out.*
- Aim your lobs toward the *backhand* side of your opponents.
- Lob down the *center* to bring on possible confusion.
- *Depth* rather than *height* is the key to an effective lob.
- Don't forget the *very high* lob.

chapter 12
The overhead

*A*uthor's Note: With the advent of better paddles *(and balls) during the last couple of decades, more "bite" or spin can now be applied to the ball. A short, lazy lob from your opposition provides you with the opportunity to <u>cut</u> the ball hard while executing your overhead.*

This is done by impacting the ball well out in front and farther to the right of where you normally meet the ball on most overheads.

Using a more toward-the-backhand grip, swipe at the ball at the 3 o'clock position with a sharp snap of the wrist. Such tremendous sidespin will cause the ball to "bounce funny" off the deck and even "funnier" as it is grabbed by the side and/or back screens.

Many cut overheads will either die on the side screen and not make it to the back screen, or will kick violently to the right as they rebound off the rear wires.

Developing a sliced overhead really rounds out your game.

The overhead is basically hit with the identical motion as its counterpart in tennis. When your opponents lob (and they will *often*, especially if you and your partner have been soundly trouncing them) as you go back for the ball, bring your paddle back to the initial phase of the overhead. Do not wait until the ball starts dropping toward you to pull your paddle back behind your head in the cocked position.

This wind-up is shorter than the more sweeping first stage of the serve. The primary reason for the more abbreviated, early wind-up is that the lob is descending from a certain height and hitting it squarely and properly calls for exact timing. Ideally you should attempt to meet the ball on your overhead when it is located slightly to your right and a little in front of you.

When possible, *jump up* to meet the descending ball and have both feet off the deck at the moment of contact. This stretching out or added height will aid you in driving the ball *downward* more sharply so that it bounces high in your opponents' court, and, hopefully, either dies in one of the back corners or kicks out unexpectedly so as to be irretrievable.

Your arm and elbow should be extended and stretched out to the limit at the moment the paddle contacts the ball. If you are hitting with a bent elbow, you are letting your opponents' lobs come down too far. The fully extended arm will also help obtain those precious, added inches of height. Try to keep the ball out in

Jones(l) and Packer (next page right) demonstrate similar and proper form while executing overheads. Their hitting arm is fully extended at

front. Making contact behind your head is awkward, difficult and tiring.

As with all platform tennis strokes, footwork is of vital importance when hitting overheads. Your weight should be evenly distributed on the *balls* of your feet. Whenever possible it is preferable to jump up for the overhead. This, obviously, calls for precise timing. It is

not easy to hit a jump overhead, and this is probably why so many players hit the ball with their feet planted firmly and flatly (and wrongly) on the platform deck. It is, however, extremely important to go up for the ball when you can. Never wait for your opponents' lob to come down to you. If you do, your body will be hunched over rather than properly stretched out, and it will be difficult for you to hit through with a smooth, flowing, non-tiring stroke.

The vast majority of overheads should be hit *gently* and *deftly,* and should be carefully aimed at the opposition's *back corners*. There is *no* reason to "smash" an overhead in platform tennis. In tennis, a powerfully smashed overhead is usually a clean

impact, and they have leaped up to the ball (feet actually left the deck) for added height.

Here Maier is jumping up and hitting down on the ball so that it lands inside the opponents' service line, then the ball begins to die deep in the back corners.

winner either in the open court or over the competition's head. In paddle, however, a hard-hit overhead will only rebound off the back screen and travel halfway back to your side of the court. Unless it is wholly unexpected, your opponents will have an easy chance at a kill. (That back screen, as mentioned earlier, is a great equalizer.)

The reason for aiming at the opposing back corners is because an almost sure winner occurs if your ball lands straight into the corner where the back and side screens meet. The ball will frequently rebound in an unpredictable manner that makes retrieval more difficult. That is to say, it will bounce either straight out and parallel to the side wire, or it will shoot out unexpectedly toward the middle of the court. Only a miraculous reflex shot will give the opposition any chance of recovery.

Occasionally a really hard-hit overhead *is* in order (four or five times during the course of an average match), but only to keep your opponents "edgy."

Change of pace in any racquet game is vital. Doing what is not expected, the unpredictable, will prevent your competition from anticipating where your ball is going. If all your overheads are aimed to bounce in the corner, your opponents will tend to stand deep in the backcourt and toward the corners. A *hard*-smashed overhead will frequently catch the opposing team off guard, and they will not be able to catch up to the ball as it rebounds far out in the court.

For the same reason, it is well to hit a few overheads (as with volleys) down the *middle* to draw them away from protecting their corners. Again, some confusion or hesitation may well occur as to who is to take the shot off the back screen.

Because there is little premium on power, the most important aspect of your paddle overhead is *consistency.* Certainly, placement is also a significant factor but secondary to steadiness and confidence when hitting the shot. An overhead hit softly that lands around the service line should be *descending* as it bounds into the back screens. That is a difficult ball to get back!

Sometimes it is hard to decide whether you or your partner should hit the overhead that is returned down the center of the court. Usually the player in the *right hand* court (ad court) should take it. He has a better view of the ball coming down the middle. He can also more quickly discern what the opponents are doing and where they are. The backhand court partner will not be backing away or moving to his left. He will be going to his right to hit the overhead, which is less

85

awkward and far easier to do for right-handed players.

A "call system," where you or your partner calls out "mine" or "yours" is imperative. The call should be *respected* and inviolate, even though one might well have to travel farther to get to the ball than his partner. Don't fight for it.

Finally, if one player on a team has a better, more consistent and accurate overhead, he should hit the majority of the returns, provided, of course, that he is in a reasonably good position to take them.

OVERHEAD RECAP:

•*Power* means little. *Placement, deftness and steadiness* are of paramount importance.

•*Jump up* toward the descending ball, and meet it with a *fully extended arm* out *front.*

•Aim the overhead toward the opponents' *back corners.*

•The partner on the *backhand* (right side of the court) should usually handle the overheads on lobs hit down the *middle.*

•*Call* (out loud) to determine who hits the overhead.

Sometimes a partnership just feels right. The above team is a "natural." The genes are right. The chemism compatible. Youth and experience blend. It's father, Dick, and son, Gary.

chapter 13
Basic doubles tactics

Author's Note: I take back what I wrote more than two decades ago in the opening few paragraphs of this chapter. While it is true that the comparative smallness of the court and the close proximity of your opponent give the player at net an inordinate advantage, a singles game can be played that is relatively enjoyable and great exercise.

In the '70s, thanks to a handful of younger players, a "national" singles championship was reinstated, and while the number of entrants has been fairly limited, the tournament has been staged each year.

Keep in mind my negative attitude toward singles might have been prejudiced somewhat by the fact that I was in my late 30s when I penned my opinions. It was (and is) a very physically demanding and tough game. I still believe doubles is a more appealing activity. If the youngsters enjoy playing singles, however, that's certainly okay with me.

In rereading this chapter on tactics some 20-plus years after writing it, there is not much I would change. Oh sure, a word here and there, but the bottom-line remains the same. Controlled power is more effective than wildly swinging away at every opportunity. Steadiness will invariably win out over flashiness. High-percentage shots, though not as satisfying, are better than the occasional, crowd-pleasing "no brainers."

There is another important thought I would like to add. Most paddle players come to the game straight from a tennis court. The usual mistake (and it figures) they make in the beginning is they bring their long, flowing, powerful tennis strokes with them. Tennis is a power game played with powerful equipment on a much larger court. It is not difficult to hit through an opponent for outright winners. On a fast, hard-surfaced tennis court two (or four) accomplished players are thought to have had a "great rally" if the ball crosses the net four or five times.

In paddle, it is not uncommon for a typical rally to last literally for minutes. A winner has to be <u>earned.</u> It has to be worked for. This takes patience and restraint. Many matches are won by attrition.

The old saw that works in practically <u>every</u> sport is particularly germane to platform tennis. Each <u>point</u> adds up to games and, ultimately, sets won. As in golf, each hole is either you against the course or (in match play) you against your opponents. Whatever happens when you hole out, remember: It is only one of 18 holes you are playing.

Handle each point as judiciously and cerebrally in paddle as a golfer contemplates each precious swing. This outlook will sustain you in close matches and will make you a tough competitor in the eyes of your opponents. It will also help you to "sneak" many victories after being on the brink of defeat.

Don't get discouraged! A shanked shot on the fairway can be offset by a scrambling next shot that runs up onto the green stiff to the pin. A lost point, game or set in paddle means little in the course of a lengthy platform tennis match unless, of course, it happens to be the final one!

Lastly and sadly, this attribute cannot be bought. It

is that unique trait that all truly great champions (in any sport) possess. I'm talking about the ability to sense what a pivotal point is, and then to be able to play it well. The great ones will be able to win that critical point 80 to 90 percent of the time.

If your partner frequently asks you what the game score is, get yourself another partner. A good player is aware at all times not only what the score is, but when it is time to play an important point. And when that "moment of truth" arises, he raises his spirits, his game, his energies to another, higher level. It is palpable and more often than not results in winning the point.

To be able to "pull your socks up," to increase your mental and physical RPMs, to hang even tougher on the crucial points, are characteristics of champions. They know what they have to do--and when--then they invariably (not all the time) do it. In other words, play the big points well–to your utmost ability. Give them your best concentration, effort and performance level. This will win titles and make adversaries wary, worried and envious.

T he last platform tennis singles tournament was played more than 30 years ago. The sport does not lend itself to any kind of fun at singles because the man at net has an overwhelming advantage over his opponent.

All kinds of handicap ideas have been suggested and tried (e.g., the server cannot come in behind his serve until his opponent has returned his ball and it bounces once, etc.), but the appeal is just not there.

Since it is impractical to play singles competitively (although you can certainly practice your strokes with your partner), you should attempt to learn as much of the basic strategy and tactics of platform tennis doubles as you can.

The Selection of Your Partner

When picking your partner, first and foremost try to find one who is at least as good as you are—preferably *better*. In addition, you should have a personality rapport with him. If you are both shy or defensive players or, on the other hand, all-out hitters, you will not make a good team. Your partner should complement you. A team consisting of two players who want to be "captain" or the star will never make a great team.

The most effective winning teams are usually composed of a daring, hard-hitter and a "steady Eddie" conservative type; an extrovert who parties it up all Saturday night while his partner is in bed by 9 p.m.; a gambler and a miser. Compatible blending of diverse personalities is just as important as putting a good forehand player with a powerful backhand player, or an excellent volleyer with a fine server.

Partners *must* get along as people, especially in a game that is played in such a confined area and has so many frustrating and tense moments. The "chemistry" must be right. So, if you are the dominant type of individual, look for a fellow who is a follower. If you are the kind that has to be led, look for a leader. No matter what, select a partner in whom you have confidence. "It takes two to tango," and there never has been a truly great doubles combination where the superior player covered 80 percent of the court. It is impractical and physically impossible.

In platform tennis doubles you will discover, for some reason or other, that you are able to play either the forehand or backhand court much better than the other side. You will rarely hear anyone say, "Smith is a tremendous, all-around performer." He is either a "tremendous forehand" or a "fine backhand" court player.

Usually with the better players, the one with the stronger backhand will be more comfortable covering the forehand court, and the person with a superior forehand will play the backhand side more adroitly. This is because in top-flight competition the majority of serves are hit down the *middle* in order to reduce the angle of the return. The person playing the forehand court, therefore, will be compelled to return many serves off his backhand, and it is essential that he have confidence in his backhand. The individual on the backhand court, however, can more readily "run around" any serves aimed at his backhand and drill a hard forehand return.

In addition, both players have their strongest ground-stroke shot when the ball is hit down the middle.

Notice the top teams in competition. Whenever they are forced to "cover" for each other by retrieving the opponents' shots in the opposite back corners, at the first opportunity they will cross back to their more familiar side of the court where they are more comfortable. It can be sad to watch a fine right-court player pinned in the left-court corner, looking as awkward as a roller skater on ice as the opposition attempts to keep him there.

For beginners, however, the general rule of thumb should be the better player should play the backhand, right, or ad side of the court. This side demands slightly more skill, and the opponents almost subconsciously will play the majority of their shots to the backhand side. Also, more "key" points will be served to the ad court. The novice will quickly decide that he somehow feels more at home on one side, and not attempt to master both sides equally.

There is some indefinable quality that the better teams seem to develop between players, and, for a lack of a better word, I call it "chemism." It is a "feeling" of knowing exactly where your partner is even if you cannot see him.

It is also a "sensing" of what shots are yours and what are his. It is knowing precisely where he will hit his shot at any given moment. This chemism is developed, and doesn't just happen. It takes years of experience under rigorous and trying competitive play.

So, as is sung in the musical, "South Pacific", "once you have found him, never let him go." Stay together and play in as many tournaments as possible. You might not find the all-important chemism with another player who seemingly is a better player. Remember, in order to be a successful team, it takes *two!*

Suggestions for Improving Doubles Play

1. When your partner is receiving serve unlike tennis, you should be back at the baseline with him. Going part of the way in, as the better tennis players do, is dangerous, and involves committing yourself needlessly. Unless your partner hits a perfect, low return, you will be caught in a most precarious and often embarrassing position. In addition, moving in can be distracting to your partner since he will spot you out of the corner of his eye.

If, on the other hand, you see that your partner has hit a fine return that will force your opponents to hit up, or to make a feeble, defensive volley, there is no reason at all why you can't charge the net and cut off their return and volley it for a winner. Remember, except when you "blitz" behind your return of serve and charge in, the rule of thumb for platform tennis strategy is that a team moves up and back *together!*

2. The partner who is winning his serve more easily and regularly should always start serving first in each set. This is allowed by the rules and just makes good sense. Perhaps the only exception is when a leftie and a rightie are paired together. There is no point in having both of you serving with the sun in your eyes when both of you can serve with the sun at your backs.

3. Whenever either you or your partner have an option or doubt as to where to hit the ball, drill your ground strokes down the *middle.* The old "center theory" has been employed successfully in lawn tennis for many years, and by many great doubles teams. This tried and true tactic works even better in platform tennis because of the closeness of the opposition, not only to you, but to each other. The chances of confusion, hesitation and uncertainty are great. It is truly the high-percentage shot.

4. When your opponents hammer the middle, who should cover the shot? After you have played with a partner for a period of time an understanding will eventually develop as to which of you protects the center area. There are three rules to follow, however, that work quite well:

a) The player who is *closest to the net* should cover a shot down the middle; the idea being that he has a better chance of "cutting off" the ball sooner.

b) The player who last hit the ball should logically be more ready to cover the return down the middle.

c) The partner on the *backhand* side should

protect the center when both members of the team are equidistant from the net. The theory here is that the backhand-court player (assuming he is right-handed) can volley better utilizing his forehand.

On lobs over the middle, the same principle holds true. The partner on the backhand side will have a better shot from a less awkward position than the player on the forehand.

5. Most of the better teams playing competitively have worked out a system of *calling* for shots—some more constantly and vociferously than others. Calling out "mine" or "yours" is an excellent idea, because the court is so small and the playing area more confined than in other racquet sports. You must establish an understanding with your partner that if one of you calls for a shot, his judgment be held inviolate. Even if you believe you have a better shot at the ball than he has, respect his call and stay away. Don't fight him for the return.

6. The more skilled players have developed a valuable asset known as "having a good eye." This is

the ability to predict practically the instant a ball leaves the opponent's paddle that it is going out of the court's playing area. A "good eye" can tell when a shot is going to be out if only by a few inches.

This ability, too, is usually obtained only after years of play. Many beginners face the problem of continually hitting "out" balls. They just cannot resist the temptation and find it extremely difficult to get their paddles out of the way in time. And how many costly points have been lost that way! If they had only dropped their paddles the point would have been theirs. It takes as much practice, as much good judgment, and just as fast reflexes to pull your paddle away as it does to get it up in order to make a fine volley.

Here again, a *calling system* will help immeasurably. If you feel a shot hit in your partner's direction is definitely going out, say (loudly), "Out!" The sound of your voice will actually *help* your partner to get his paddle out of the path of the ball— it's a signal that seems to *trigger* his reflexes. It is truly

97

amazing how this works.

Obviously, as with calling "mine" or "yours," you must develop faith in your partner's eye, and he in yours. When you reach that stage it will be worth at least one point a game to you, since most players hit that many out-balls in a match. Letting an out-ball go is tantamount to a walk in baseball. What easier way to get on first base, or win a point?

7. Generally speaking, you should lob frequently, drop volley rarely, and drop shot never. When you have a sure putaway, (if there is any such thing in platform tennis), put it away. Don't hit the hard shot. Go for the obvious, certain winner.

8. Vary your return of serve and disguise it as much as you can. *Hold* all your shots as long as you can. This will prevent the opponents from anticipating where you plan to hit the ball. *Change of pace* and *steadiness* are the keys to winning platform tennis, not overwhelming power.

9. When your partner is serving and you are at the net, poach occasionally. You will be able to hit a few winning volleys. Your opponents will be extra careful on their returns, and you will be helping your partner win his serve. Remember, a person's serve is apt to be only as successful as his net man is. In this game, of all racquet sports, it takes *two* to win. A "singles star" will be a lonely loser!

10. Do not, whatever you do, ever glare at your partner or moan when he misses an easy shot, or fails to get that big point for you. He is doing his very best and really wants to win as badly as you do. Pat him on the back and tell him to "forget it." And mean it. There will be other big points and important matches. Show him that you have complete faith in him and his ability. To play winning platform tennis you must

Move as team with the ball. Note players i foregroun have bot moved to the right becaus the opponer playing a dee shot from the backhan corner has n chance hitting sharply angle shot cros cour

Same is tr whe opponent forehar court returnin Team foregrou has mov together the le have as much confidence in your partner's game as your own. It behooves you not to shake your partner's concentration or display any frustration.

11. Don't allow "close calls" against you, or "let cords" that drop over on your side of the court, to discourage you. It truly is amazing how these adverse breaks tend to even out over the course of a match.

12. When you and your partner have pulled one of your opponents wide over to the backhand (right) court and you are both at net, your concern should be to cover your forehand alley and the center, leaving your backhand alley relatively open. The reverse holds true on a wide ball to your opponents' forehand (left) court. By so doing, you will be "cutting off" the angled return. It is very unlikely that they can hit such a wide cross-court angle for a winner from such an off-the-court position. In other words "float" or flow in the direction

of the ball.

13. Never change a winning style, and always change a losing one. There is an old proverb that says: "Never change horses in midstream." That statement might be amended with "unless the horse is losing ground to the current."

If you are being severely thrashed by a team you feel you should beat, have a little conference with your partner as you change sides on the odd game. Discuss between yourselves what you have been doing wrong, and decide how you plan to change your tactics.

Perhaps you are not being aggressive enough, or perhaps the circumstances call for steadiness. You might be playing the stronger of your two opponents, or even worse you are not hammering away at their weaknesses.

It is just not enough to say, "Come on, let's get hot." It is not always that easy to pull your games together and to "get up." The mark of a good doubles team is one that can find and exploit the opponents' weaknesses and eventually win the match even when they are having an off day.

Try to keep your eyes on your partner. Know where he or she is and move accordingly. Don't look straight ahead when your partner is behind you.

14. When a southpaw and a right-handed player are paired up it is usually best for the leftie to play the right side of the court. This statement

100

assumes the two players are about equal in ability. It is, generally, easier for most players to return shots rebounding from the side and/or back screens off the forehand. This capability more than offsets the possible problems encountered when covering shots down the middle with two backhands.

15. Faithfully employ and practice the fundamental strokes set forth in this book. Don't regress to that old grip or old stroke you have been using for years just because you and your partner find yourselves behind. The principles promulgated in the earlier chapters are sound and will improve your game as long as you practice them—both in "fun" matches as well as under the pressure of competition.

16. The best advice I can offer to a beginner is to *study the styles* of the top players in the game today. This book gives you sound instructions relative to the basic fundamentals and strategy of platform tennis, but everyone still has his own unique and individualized style that seems to work for him. Watch the more adroit competitors play, analyze their strengths, and attempt to emulate the things they do especially well. They might just work for you, too.

Classic scene at the 1992 Nationals: jam-packed galleries; hospitality tent; crisp, clear early spring weather, and extended rallies– a purrfect paddle day!

chapter 14
Competitive mixed doubles

Author's Note: I honestly cannot believe how chauvinistic I was in my middle 30s! Or was it the era when men were men and women either liked it that way or tolerated us? I don't know.

This time around I was tempted not to include this chapter because its tone is rather supercilious, and my attitude (in the 1960s. . . no longer) toward women on the paddle court was demeaning.

I decided to keep the chapter in as is— (or was), because, frankly, I would not change the basic advice and strategies advocated for mixed doubles. It still holds true. Aging has (and should have) mellowed me, however, and I probably hold greater respect for women per se than I did 25-plus years ago.

In addition, while attending the 1992 national mixed and national women's doubles tournaments (held at Beden's Brook in Princeton, N.J., and Huntington Country Club on Long Island), I discovered firsthand that today's female paddler can very effectively (thank you!) hold up her side of the paddle court. She is also more aggressive than her predecessor was in the '60s and '70s, and, at the top level of play, there is no way to "rattle" or intimidate her. As a matter of fact, she welcomes being challenged.

Mixed doubles has become a far better form of competition than it was, mainly because the women have improved immensely, and the base of highly skilled females has become so much broader.

Paddle players come in all sizes. David Ohlmuller and Patty Hogan were finalists in the 1992 Nationals held at Beden's Brook in Princeton, N.J.

N o book on platform tennis could possibly be considered complete without a chapter on the subject of mixed doubles (troubles?).

Platform tennis is the only bat and ball sport in which the female partner has an excellent opportunity to hold her own. If she is proficient off the screens, is content to allow her partner to cover as much of the

104

court as he possibly can and concentrates primarily on being steady when protecting her own territory, she is well along the way to becoming a most desirable and effective mixed-doubles player.

In *most* cases (certainly not all the time) the woman is the weaker member of the team. She must, therefore, realize that she will be tormented, hit at, and played unmercifully by her opponents. She must be prepared to accept this punishment good naturedly as being part of the game. She has to rise to the challenge.

There is nothing more disconcerting than being unable to wear down the distaff member of the opposing team. Undramatic *steadiness* rather than occasional sensational shotmaking should be the woman's strategy in a competitive mixed-doubles match.

The better women players today are a level above the others not because of their power or their ability to hit devastating, clean winners. They are effective because of their willingness to display restraint, patience, and tenacity. A good female partner is one who does not want to hog the limelight. She is content to let her male partner be the aggressive and exciting shotmaker.

In addition to this basic understanding, there are other key strategies and tactics to be employed. And for all of them we have assumed that the man is the stronger player:

1. The male should play the *backhand* side of the court. It is the more difficult side from which to return serve, the screen play is harder to master, and more important "key points" are made or saved from the right or ad court. There are also more opportunities for winners. It is easier for the male to hit the opponents' lobs from the backhand court, and he will cover shots

down the middle with his forehand ground strokes and/or volleys.

2. The man should start serving *first*. In this game you should ignore the tradition of chivalry. Emily Post obviously never played competitive paddle mixed doubles when she advocated "ladies first." The man should serve first even if it means his partner will have to serve with the sun in her eyes.

By being the first to serve, the odds are that he will have the opportunity of serving *more times* than his partner.

3. When the woman is serving, the man should "poach" (cross over toward the middle and attempt to pick off the return of serve) often—far more frequently than would be considered prudent in men's doubles.

This tactic will harass and disconcert the opposition, and will help his partner hold her serve. It will, of course, work better when the female is serving to her counterpart rather than to the opposing gentleman.

4. As a rule of thumb, the male should be prepared to take *all* the shots hit down the middle (it will also be his forehand). There should never be any doubt or hesitation (or quibbling) as to who should hit

Young David
Ohlmuller
displaying rarely
seen two-handed
backhand and
one-handed
forehand while
partner Patty
Hogan is right
there at his elbow.

a particular ball. The answer is an unequivocal *"the man!"*

5.   A very effective shot for the man to hit, especially early in the match, is a hard return of serve right at the opposing female at net. Even if she ducks and the ball goes soaring out of the court, much has been accomplished. This is tantamount to a pitcher "dusting back" a batter in baseball. She will quickly realize you are playing to win, that beneath the gallant veneer there lies a burning desire to be victorious at almost any cost, and the "edginess" you have instilled in her will remain. Needless to say, such a ploy will be worth many points during the course of the match.

This shot should not be made with the intent of physically harming the woman. Such intimidation, however, is a good strategy to use in the early stages of a match.

6. As mentioned earlier the greatest asset the woman can offer her male partner is *steadiness.* This does *not* mean she should lob every shot back or "poop ball" every return. It merely suggests that she should make every effort to reduce her *errors* to an absolute minimum. Many more points are lost because of costly errors than are won because of occasional crowd-pleasing winners. This is especially true of platform tennis, where a clean winner is far more difficult to make than in most racquet sports. It has been calculated that *70 to 80 percent* of all *points scored* in paddle are made on *errors, not winners.* *Steadiness* and *consistency* are the two most important words to remember while competing in a paddle match.

7. A warning is in order for the men. It is well to keep in mind that the male partner will see very few balls coming in his direction. He will have to stand by helplessly and watch his partner lunge, twist and puff as she doggedly returns shot after shot.

Such a scene will ignite an inherent urge in the male to rush to his damsel's aid. He will edge slowly toward her side of the court hoping one of the opponents' balls will be placed near enough to him to get his paddle on it and put a quick end to his partner's distress. What happens?

a) Usually he is not in the proper position and he makes a weak return, or

b) He has left his side of the court completely unguarded and the opponents volley a clean winner away in his unprotected corner, or

c) He will have the natural tendency to over-compensate—to try to do too much with the shot and, hence, an error results.

So, the man must also be patient. He must not try

to do too much with the few balls that come in his direction. He should have the absolute confidence in his female partner's ability to withstand the barrage. He should be buttressed with the thought that on the next point they might well have the opposing female pinned in her corner. It is all part of the wonderful, fun and frustrating game of mixed doubles.

8. An effective tactic for the man to employ when the female opponent is serving is to "blitz," or go to net behind his return. Nothing will undermine the woman's confidence, or frustrate her partner at the net, more than banging a low, hard return of serve right at the girl coming to net behind her delivery. And, remember, she must come to net. She has no choice. Innumerable faults will usually occur because she will be trying to hit a serve a little deeper or a little harder than would be necessary if she did not have the pressure of a "blitzer" to contend with.

9. Lobbing a return of serve directly over the female's head can undermine the opposing man's confidence in his ability to serve well and still cover the court. Unlike in tennis, it is practically impossible to kill a lob with an overhead smash. If you lob purposefully, the man who has just served and is coming to net will have to cross over behind his partner and make a high, weak defensive volley.

10. Finally, keep in mind that mixed doubles is a thwarting game that demands the utmost patience and a willingness by both partners to "hang on" and "ride out" the many moments of anguish. Be prepared for the lost opportunities and the frustrations, and you will be a far better and happier mixed-doubles player.

These points of strategy are to be used when playing *competitive* platform tennis mixed doubles. You can be much more chivalrous as well as frivolous when you and your spouse are playing your regular Saturday morning game at the local club against neighbors–especially if the neighbor's wife is attractive.

MIXED DOUBLES RECAP:

1. The woman should afford her male partner every opportunity to be the "hero." Her prime responsibilty is to be *steady* and *errorless*.

2. The man should play the *backhand* side of the court, and should *always* serve first.

3. The man should attempt to cut off as many shots as he can while his partner is serving. He should also cover *all* shots coming down the middle.

4. An early-in-the-match ploy is to drive a shot right at the female opponent. The purpose of this tactic is to rattle but not hurt her.

5. The man should frequently "blitz" when returning the opposing woman's serve. When the opposition's male is serving, a lob over the *woman's* head is a winning and disconcerting tactic.

chapter 15
Love set

*A*uthor's Note: Thanks to the kind permission of the author, I am allowed to include in this book a reprint of "LOVE SET." It was included in *THE OTHER RACQUET SPORTS*, published in 1978 by the McGraw-Hill Book Company.

It is appropriate because the vignette took place on a paddle court, and it is a true story.

The author was Dick Squires.

I have played competitive platform tennis since 1963. Who could accurately estimate how many times my wooden paddle has spanked that spongy orange ball across the net, or how often I've dug one low off the wires? The total count would boggle the innards of the most sophisticated calculator. I was fortunate enough to win more than my share of "loot." And along the way I've made many friends, and I have pleasant memories that will endure for a lifetime. One of the most unforgettable thrills I have ever experienced "on the boards," however, occurred just recently. It was a competitive match I will always remember.

What a gorgeous Sunday afternoon it was! The air was clear and crisp. As my partner and our opponents trudged toward the court, the snow made crunchy noises under our sneakers. The uniformly deep-blue sky was only occasionally interrupted by wispy clouds, and the mercury in the warming hut's thermometer shivered in the teens. For platform tennis aficionados, it was perfect paddle weather.

It was a rare treat for me to be playing on a Sunday afternoon. I had been married for more than 17 years (divorced five years before) and that "day of rest" usually reserved for work around the house and visits to the in-laws was now mine to do with as I pleased. A divorce, albeit expensive, does offer new freedom, although, oddly enough, one can miss the menial and mundane chores of the "head of the family." And if there are children in a marriage, a divorce can be especially painful. At any rate, back to this memorable match.

My pretty, blonde paddle partner and I found ourselves struggling against a well-balanced pair that had youth, stamina, and quick reflexes working in their favor. But then we had my experience (I was the oldest player on the court by 25 years!) and my teammate's alacrity. And our combined determination was at least equal to that of those across the net.

We divided the first four games, with the guys holding serves and the gals dropping theirs. (Not unlike most mixed doubles paddle encounters.) When the women were up at the net, they volleyed every ball they could reach without having to move more than six inches in any direction. The rest of the court had to be covered somehow by the men. (Not unlike most mixed doubles paddle encounters.) Neither of the women had the faintest concept of screen play, so the teams were evenly matched in that area. (Not unlike most mixed doubles paddle encounters.)

With unexpected suddenness, the opposition broke my serve, thereby rendering a severe blow to my ego and our chances of winning the set. (The guy just cannot afford to lose his serve in mixed-doubles competition.) As we changed court sides, the opposing male, a tall, tow-headed, flat-stomached youth of 21, remarked to me out of the corner of his mouth, "Didn't think we'd take that big serve, eh? Now you're in serious trouble." I didn't need this big fella to tell me that!

His attractive, full-bosomed, brown-haired teammate had already peeled off her down vest, and her abundant endowment was readily evident beneath her bright, orange turtleneck. She smiled innocently at me, but somehow I had the distinct feeling that she had put him up to making that nerve-racking comment.

My pixyish partner sidled over to me as we returned to the court, and through tightly clenched lips vowed, "Don't worry. We'll get 'em. Don't get discouraged." (She obviously did not know me very well. I never give up.) Then she winked at me and I felt it down to my sneakers.

Buttressed by these words of encouragement, I felt invigorated and hopeful once again. And, sure enough, after two successful "blitzes," a fault, and a well-placed lob over the brunette's outstretched paddle, we had broken the big fella's service at love! The score was deadlocked at three games.

The time had now come to "break" my partner's serve, which in mixed doubles really means to have her win it for once. We could then exchange court sides with the lead ours. My diminutive teammate bravely tried, but it was in vain. The adversaries pounced on her "fat" serve and twice returned balls she could not volley back. In an effort to help her on the next point, I prematurely tried to poach and was cleanly passed down my vacant alley. This was followed by a fault, and as quickly as you can say "paddle tennis is not platform tennis," we were behind again, four games to three.

The rawboned, sinewy male across the net wore a mile-long smirk across his face. He was the essence of unabashed cockiness, displaying the poise and killer instinct of a front runner who is beginning to taste victory. We hadn't had too much difficulty taking his partner's delivery the first time around, but she was serving more boldly. Hitting in four of five deep serves and making us move to return them, she ultimately won the game at 15. We were down three games to five.

Even though we were now in pretty dire straits, for just an instant my concentration deserted me, which can be disastrous in any competitive match. I found myself staring at the voluptuous, sparkling, young woman across the net awaiting my serve. She was a "slick-looking chick," with chocolate-tanned skin to blend with her almond-colored eyes. I wondered if she looked so healthy from playing paddle every day or from weekend skiing trips, or had she just gotten back from some Caribbean island? The stretch pants she wore were molded tightly to her seat and legs like an extra layer of skin. She was, needless to say, quite disconcerting and I felt like the proverbial "dirty old man!"

Her partner had the lean physique of a regular, serious jogger. He reminded me of a model that Norman Rockwell would have selected for a World War II poster that encouraged kids to "Join the Marines." I think I hated him at that moment!

My teammate was tiny and a good deal younger than our adversaries, but displayed the eagerness of a tour "rabbit." I was proud of the way she would "hang in there," continuing to paste the ball boldly despite our being down. She never once resorted to "poop-balling" in the hope our competitors would start making foolish errors. She was playing to win rather than not to lose, and there is a tremendous difference!

I took a deep breath and began to serve the ninth game. It went to a deuce-ad situation several times before we reluctantly bowed to defeat, six games to three, on what I want the entire world to know was a very lucky screen shot that landed in the deep corner crease and rebounded unpredictably.

What was so memorable about this particular set of paddle? Well, now I will tell you. When we ran to net and began shaking hands (in the proper platform tennis tradition) a chorus of voices from the other three competitors greeted me with, "Nice playing, Dad!"

It was the first time all three of my children, Gary, Cathy and Pam, had been interested enough in platform tennis (and me!) to play the game together. How the years had raced by! How grown up they had all become. How much I had missed their daily presence since 1973, when their mother and I separated. And you can imagine how much love I felt for them at that very special moment.

Dad with, from left, Cathy, Gary and Pam in 1975.

Circa 1990. How the years have raced by!

chapter 16
Timeless tips

Over the course of almost 50 years of playing competitive racquet sports, I have established a fairly extensive list of "timeless tips" that have worked often enough to be classified as axiomatic. They have endured the test of time.

Without attempting to put them in any particular order, or to rank them by their importance, here are some proven suggestions that have been valuable to me:

•Usually the seventh game of a set and the third point of a game are the most pivotal and, therefore, important to do what it takes to try and win them. What is the most important point of any match? The *last* one!

•The stronger partner of a doubles tandem should play the backhand or ad side of the court.

•There are critical "big points" that occur in close paddle contests. These points should be nurtured carefully and not blithely "blown" by trying silly, low-percentage shots. You should mentally and physically raise your game and do everything you can to win these points.

•*Patience*, particularly on a paddle court, is a virtue. This does *not* mean being a wimp and always playing defensively. It just means biding your time and waiting for an opening before going for a winner. Playing in containment and being steady will win the majority of platform tennis encounters.

When playing "just for fun," try to simulate tournament conditions. While top-flight competitors do seem to have the ability to play perceptibly better in tournaments, and continue to improve in the latter rounds, they usually play hard when practicing. By so doing, they are able to "get into a match" quicker than people who "goof around" when playing non-competitive, fun paddle.

•Each point is an individual match. And that is the way to play it. Although you hit many more balls during a paddle match than on a golf course (hopefully!), every stroke, as on the course, taken on the court should be hit with a *purpose* in mind. There is a *reason* behind every lob, every wicked forehand, every carefully placed volley and overhead. Frantic, wild swipes at the ball result in more errors and lost points than winners.

•Changes of pace and a *variety* of shotmaking and returns are like a boxer's jabs. They keep the opponent wary and off-balance. The best opportunity to employ this strategy is on the return of serve. While your "bread and butter" return is an aggressive, hard hit forehand (or occasional backhand), a sharply angled, soft dink, or a lob over either the oncoming server's or his up-at-net partner's head can be very effective. So can a once-in-a-while, down the alley drive that keeps the person at net edgy and not too prone to poach. Doing the unpredictable, however, does *not* mean hitting "crazy" no (or low) percentage shots.

•Think *positively,* particularly when serving. The single serve can be a stultifying experience, even for the most adroit paddler. When it is 4-5 in the third set and your turn to serve, during the changeover concentrate on the basics. You have been serving well. Your partner has been cutting off many of the opponents' returns. Do not let up on your serve because you don't want to fault. Better players will kill a poopy serve. If you are going to become a "better player," you have to keep hitting your serve with authority—even if it means some painful faults at times. If you are content with just putting the ball in play, you will always remain a mediocre "club B player."

•Before you are scheduled to play a match, don't watch another match. As a matter of fact, try to get away from other players who are talking about paddle, or a match they just completed. In other words, don't vicariously play points when you are away from the court. There are enough points to be played in an actual match. When you are between contests, relax. Don't even think paddle.

•Don't brood over lost opportunities, or the previous point you lost on a net cord, or a set-up kill that you blew. That point is gone forever. Invariably net cords even out during the course of any match. We all commit easy errors. Forget them. Remember: Every point is a separate match unto itself. If you win the majority of them, chances are you'll win the match.

•While I was never an athlete who subjected my body to a rigorous training routine when in my prime, now, at 60-plus, I do believe in the value of exercise, clean living and moderation in the "evil habits."

More than anything, try to stretch, loosen up and warm up before playing a serious, competitive paddle contest. This is especially important because our sport is frequently played in wintry weather. Some pre-game stretching of all body parts, perhaps a few moments of running in place will stand you in good stead when you get out on the boards.

•Much has been written about an athlete's "killer instinct." Are you born with it, or can it be cultivated? Can you be a nice person and still be a killer in the sports arena? My personal feeling is that in *most* people it *can* be developed. The ability to excel in the din of intense competition, to elevate your overall on-court performance for the "big matches," the thriving on pressure points can be taught and learned and practiced.

Sports Science, a relatively new brand of athletic training and development, is proving that mental and physical abilities can, indeed, be enhanced through specific, scientific methodology.

The "killer instinct" is nothing more than an amalgamation of the various points mentioned in this chapter. "Going for the jugular," "playing all the points as though they were precious," "hitting the majority of your shots with a purpose," "not letting up or coasting," and "girding yourself to play the big points especially well," all combine to create a portrait of a competitor who possesses the wonderful and essential trait, a "killer instinct."

•It is important to start off in any racquet/paddle sport *correctly.* If you truly study and implement the basics of strokemaking and strategy suggested in this book, you will, guaranteed, experience rapid improvement and, thereby, enjoy playing the sport sooner. The better you become in something, the more you like it. That is an irrefutable cliche that has withstood the test of time. The key is to start employing the *proven* fundamentals ASAP. There aren't too many professional platform tennis instructors around these days, so it is easy to develop bad habits when you first take up the sport. If you are a tennis player, you'll most likely be hitting your ground strokes too hard and will have a difficult time with screen play. Your intuitive tendency will be to cut off all balls deep in the court before they bound into the wires. Wrong!

If you have played either squash or racquetball, you will undoubtedly have a good, early "feel" for screen angles, but your wristy ground strokes just won't work consistently.

Platform tennis has its very own unique strokes and tactics. From the beginning they should be employed and practiced. Read, study and re-read this little book. It will provide you with the best jump-start possible.

•Get into your opponents' head(s). I am not suggesting you do anything unsportsmanlike, but there are some subtle things you can do (or say) that can help. For instance, when warming up, pay close attention to your opponent's strengths and, more important, his weaknesses. He really bangs his forehand, hits it with confidence and a lot of topspin. He actually runs around his backhand, and when you finally get one to his backhand he returns it rather feebly. Check his form and effectiveness as he practices screen shots. Does he ever "rip one," or are all his returns lobs? That will tell you something.

Is he comfortable up at net volleying? Does he meet the ball out front with a firm wrist. Does he volley in a specific, controlled manner, or is he hesitant and flat on his feet? How close does he stand to the net? Such observations made during the warm-up will be helpful to you and your partner after the game begins.

•Most of the racquet and paddle sports are as much mental as they are physical. One of the best "gamesmanship" ploys I ever made (that really worked) occurred in the finals of the 45s nationals in 1983. My partner, Bill Mimnaugh, was serving 3-5 in the deciding set after we had split 7-6 tie-breakers. We were down 15-40, two match points. Bill was struggling. I ambled back to the baseline and put my arms around him. "Come on," I said warmly. "If you want to have a story to tell your grandchildren someday, we gotta' pull this match out." He nodded and smiled and we proceeded, with some difficulty, to eke out that crucial game.

As we changed sides I casually muttered to the guy who was going to serve out the match at 5-4, "Boy! I'm glad I'm not serving this game." (We hadn't even come close to breaking his serve during the entire match.) He gave me a classic double-take, then shook his head rather incredulously. Had I really said that to him?

He went back to serve and promptly hit consecutive faults. We went on to annex the game and eventually the final set and match 7-6 (9-7).

Was my humorous (?) comment an unfair tactic? I don't believe it was. I was, after all, semi-kidding. *Semi*-kidding, that is. My remark had reminded him that he was supposed to be feeling pressure.

Inside of five critical minutes, with my words I had relaxed my partner and unnerved the opponent. Good show!

•Developing self-confidence can only occur when you realize it is inevitable that you're going to make some errant shots during the course of any match. Ben Hogan, the legendary golfer of the 1940s and '50s, once said, "I have never played a perfect round of golf. I've always hit a few bad shots." It is okay to strive for perfection, but it just cannot be attained— particularly on a paddle court where you might hit *several thousand* balls during a competitive contest.

Self-confidence comes as you play and practice and improve. A self-confident player makes the game look easy and appears to be having fun. He or she has "been there before," has faced pivotal, pressure-packed moments, has "met triumph and disaster and treated both impostors the same."

Self-confidence, combined with *partner-*confidence, makes for a very tough platform tennis team.

Now you know all my secrets. Good luck!

chapter 17

An historic "first"

uthor's Note: This heretofore unpublished essay was written on November 18, 1973. Why does it belong in this book almost 20 years after the event took place? Because, in some ways, the Vat Gold Cup was a significant turning point in the history of platform tennis, and here is the only document that accurately depicts the happening. It was authored by a person who was there—who played a lead role. Me!

Just two years later Charles Millard and the Coca Cola Bottling Company of New York approached the APTA with the idea of a Tribuno (vermouth) professional paddle circuit. Imagine playing the country club, elitist game for money!

I would like to believe this unique tournament, staged for the first time in the South, with the top teams competing for money ($10,000) for the first time, and shown on national television for the first time, paved the way and helped accelerate the growth of paddle that occurred in the mid-'70s.

The excitement and apprehension I felt is fun to look back on and, hopefully, this accounting will vicariously provide readers with the feeling of "being there," of witnessing firsthand when paddle "went public" for the first time.

Even today as I re-read the manuscript I tingle. It was a supreme moment, a marvelous opportunity and great exposure for our little game.

We now own a home on Hilton Head Island, S.C.

Every time we go down there for a few days of vacation, I invariably find a moment to visit Sea Pines Plantation. There is now a golf driving range where we installed the four-court paddle complex. The courts have long since been removed and scrapped. Apparently after the tournament took place and the "best players in the world" had departed, no one remained behind to promote the sport, to create a paddle program, and to sustain interest and activity.

Such a sad ending, however, does not diminish the achievement. In November of 1973, on an idylic island in the Southern low country, platform tennis had its moment in the sun.

November 18, 1973
THE VAT GOLD
PLATFORM TENNIS CHAMPIONSHIPS

It was approximately 1:15 in the afternoon when I turned and walked away from that beautiful scene. Behind me the players were warming up in preparation for the final round of the First Vat Gold Cup Men's Platform Tennis Championship.

The climate was unseasonably cool for November 11 on Hilton Head Island, S.C.—around 40 degrees, which, of course, the purists would call ideal "paddle" weather.

Five flags fluttered noisily above the scoreboard and their flamboyant colors stood out against the perfectly blue cloudless sky.

The bleachers were rapidly filling up with spectators—some ardent aficionados of platform tennis, but most were completely uninitiated to the attractive appeals and subtle nuances of this great, but little known, racquet and ball sport. An aura of excitement and anticipation was felt by everyone, players and viewers alike. There was an unmistakable feeling that this particular day, this particular match, this entire event represented an historic milestone in the 45-year history of platform tennis.

The months of hard work and planning preceding the tournament, the myriad of details and the overcoming of seemingly insurmountable problems now seemed worth it. It would be impossible to describe the explosive feeling of personal satisfaction I was experiencing at that special moment. I *had* to leave because the entire scene, and all its potential implications, were just too much.

I trudged rather wearily back to the posh Sea Pines Plantation villa, peeled off my soggy playing togs (my partner, Doug Russell, and I had just won the consolation title), and climbed into the bathtub to mollify my protesting 42-year-old muscles. Keeping the hot-water tap slightly open, I put my feet up on the wall tiles and closed my eyes. In the distance I could hear the occasional patter of applause following some well-executed stroke or extended rally. "It really happened!" I screamed out to the empty apartment. "Squires! You pulled it off!"

A mere three months before I had received a phone call from Joseph Tomassi, vice president of International Operations at National Distillers. He wanted me to come in to New York City to explore how a division of his company, Munson Shaw, could develop some kind of kinship with the fast-growing, but ultraconservative sport of platform tennis. The fact that "the large numbers weren't there" when compared to, say, tennis (150,000 paddlers versus 12 million tennis players, 3,000 platform tennis decks versus an estimated 140,000 regular tennis courts) did not seem to faze him. The demographics and the "undiluted, thoroughbred qualities" of platform tennis participants and devotees were, however, most attractive factors as he wanted to promote a high quality Scotch (Vat 69 Gold). The present paddlers are a fairly elegant, discriminating, "waspy" lot—kind of what white-flanneled amateur tennis players were a quarter of a century ago.

He also envisioned "paddle" as being an appealing, sleeping giant ready to explode as America's next popular, year-round, family participation sport. I agreed with him! And perhaps even more significant, these inherent appealing features are *proven.* The paddler, regardless of his or her degree of proficiency, is utterly addicted to and in love with the sport of platform tennis. To them it is more than just a game— it is a way of life.

After discussing several possible concepts with Mr. Tomassi, the idea of a sort of "Masters Classic" tournament emerged. That is, the best 16 doubles teams in the country would be invited to compete for the Vat 69 Gold Cup—a natural and prestigious name for the event.

Because I am under contract to Mark McCormack's firm (International Management Group), which handles the business affairs of such outstanding athletes as Arnold Palmer, Janet Lynn, Rod Laver, Pele, etc., I contacted IMG's Dick Alford, the individual who has the dubious pleasure and challenge of representing Dick Squires, "Mr. Platform Tennis," or otherwise also dubbed "the fading Golden Boy of Paddle." I told him of my conversation with Mr. Tomassi and he contributed some additional ideas—the most exciting of which was to try to get the tournament national television exposure!

Then it had to be decided where the event should be held. For several months I had tried to convince Charles Fraser, president of the Sea Pines Company, that platform tennis was a sport to be played in warm as well as cold climate areas. His interest had been whetted, but my company, Sports Marketing Associates Corporation, had not received any orders for any Squires Modular court installations. The development he started on Hilton Head in 1956 seemed like a natural site, and it would be a perfect way to introduce the sport not only to Sea Pines' property owners, but also to the entire South for the first time.

I called Charles and informed him of our plans. He was extremely amiable to the whole idea, especially when the possibility of nationwide television exposure (for his development) was mentioned!

Several precious weeks of tense contract negotiations ensued with Sea Pines, National Distillers and CBS, and oftentimes it appeared the entire deal might fall through because of some minor hassles (like how much it was going to cost!), but finally contracts were signed. The all-important television commitment, which obviously was of prime importance to all parties, did not become a reality until just prior to the start of the tournament. Highlights of the event will be shown some time this winter in a 35-minute segment on CBS's "Sports Spectacular".

Richly engraved invitations were sent out to the players, and acceptances were received from 11 of the top-ranking 16 teams invited, which must be some kind of a record. Admittedly, we had offered them unique enticements—all their expenses were paid (for spouses and friends), and the victorious team was to win a free trip to Europe! Not a bad prize for a bunch

129

of hardworking executives who represent probably the last of today's "true blue" amateurs in the world of sport.

I flew down to Hilton Head 48 hours before the players were scheduled to arrive. There were still a thousand and one details to cover—certainly not the least of which was to make certain the four-court "Paddle Center" was finished on time.

Upon arriving I immediately went to the location of the courts and saw (by moonlight), much to my chagrin, that they were only three-quarters on their way toward completion. Needless to say, I experienced a few hours of untroubled sleep that night! It is rather difficult to play championship platform tennis matches on courts lacking tightened screens, lines or a net.

Very early the following morning I aroused my field superintendent and let it be known under no uncertain terms what had to be done, how much the tournament meant to which people, what the consequences would be if the courts weren't ready, and that I was extremely unhappy with the job being done.

By mid-morning the courts were being swarmed over by industrious carpenters, painters and long-haired unskilled "lifters and backs." Lighting fixtures were attached to their power source to facilitate working around the clock in the unlikely event this would be necessary—and it turned out to be *not* so unlikely.

Competitors arrived late the following evening and were sound asleep completely oblivious to the frantic, last-minute work being done on the courts in order to prepare them for play (practice) the following (Friday) morning. If it had rained (and the weather forecaster

130

persisted in predicting it), we never would have made it. As it was, the finishing touches were applied to the courts around 2:30 Friday morning, and a mere six hours later they were filled by the players eager to loosen up and prepare for the tournament the subsequent day. It was a real cliffhanger!

There were other things to worry about. Very little publicity had gone out to the local press and to people living at Sea Pines. Programs had to be written and printed for distribution throughout the island—posters created and placed in key areas. Such publicity should have been done weeks before, but there were apparently still many skeptics at Sea Pines who believed platform tennis was a cold-weather sport to be played only in 20-degree weather. They didn't want to have anything to do with a possible "loser." (These are the same type of narrow-minded individuals who believed 30 years ago that tennis was only to be played outdoors on clear, warm days, and on grass! How wrong they were!) Somehow these nitty-gritty projects were all accomplished before the matches began.

On Saturday morning an amazing thing happened. A massive cold front moved in the day the First Vat Gold Cup Platform Tennis Championship was to commence. The temperature plunged to 35 degrees and the winds were whipping across the courts in gusts of up to 25 knots. Ah, *perfect* "paddle" weather—or so the traditionalists would claim. It was as if I had ordered the weather to make the "Yankee Paddlers" feel right at home.

All the matches were run off quite smoothly that opening day and the four top-seeded and favored teams advanced to the semifinals. Word was spreading around the island that this "new game" of platform tennis was great fun and exciting to watch—not a

"Mickey Mouse version of tennis" after all. During the day the number of spectators steadily grew, and even the entirely unknowing seemed to be enjoying the suspenseful action and skill of the players.

So much an integral part of platform tennis is the apres "paddle" social activities. This is one of the primary reasons why hundreds of courts are being installed today at country clubs. They keep the clubs open and utilized on a 12-month basis.

Then, too, the paddler is rather like the golfer or skier. He, or she, enjoys the camaraderie and conviviality after ramming in the final putt or making that last run down the slopes.

National Distillers held a bash of a cocktail party Saturday night at its beautiful ocean-front villa. This was followed by a gala dinner at Sea Pines' Plantation

Actor Gary Merrill (right) helped make the draw in Vat Gold Cup

Club. In the attractive dining room, actor Gary Merrill, a recent convert to the game, entertained us during the dinner by reading some humorous and poignant poems written by children. He also told a funny story about his 10-year marriage to actress Bette Davis. One of the reasons it finally ended in divorce was that he just couldn't get used to being called "Petah" when he was making love to her!

Innumerable speeches were given during the course of the evening, and everyone had a memorable, mirth-filled time. Denis Wilde, director of Vat 69, a charming and delightful Britisher, said he had instantly fallen madly in love with the game and that he hoped next year's Vat Gold Cup could be played in *London!* (The only courts presently located outside the U.S. are an isolated few in Japan, Poland, Italy and Germany). "After all," he said, "we gave you tennis. Why shouldn't you return the favor by introducing us to platform tennis? I think it's a better game!"

Next morning's semifinals were a couple of beauties. The second-seeded team of Chum Steele and Keith Jennings, from Massachusetts, were upset in four sets by New Jersey's fourth-ranked Baird brothers, Chip and Steve, who are in their early 20s. (Their father also competed in this tournament, which certainly proves platform tennis is truly a sport of a lifetime!) The current U.S. champions, John Mangan and Bob Kingsbury had to go all out to defeat the third seeded John Beck and Herb Fitzgibbon, also in four close sets.

IMG's Jay Michaels, who was directing the filming of the action for CBS, seemed elated with his camera crew's efforts. They were shooting the play from every conceivable angle, from a specially erected, 100-foot high tower, through the screening and by lifting up the snowgates (which should probably be given a more appropriate name for courts in the South!) located around the base of the court in order to capture the "scrambling and digging" of the players retrieving low balls in the back corners.

Jay said he felt it was a more exciting sport to watch than regular tennis–although somewhat harder to film. It appeared, however, that platform tennis' television debut was going to be a successful one, and for the first time the game would be properly filmed and viewed by millions of Americans. Soon there would be a demand for thousands of courts—at colleges, in public parks, at every hotel and motel—and I'd be rich!

"Yeow!!" I had dosed off in the tub and one of my feet had fallen directly under the still-flowing hot water tap. A rapid return to reality resulted, and I jumped out and quickly dressed.

Returning to the court site was like Paradise revisited. The championship match was in progress and the gallery was intently following every tense, prolonged point. My "babies" (the courts) looked as though they had been there for years. Freshly installed shrubs ringed the perimeter of the structures, and gorgeous yellow (or were they Vat Gold?) chrysanthemums had been planted in giant wooden flower boxes in the gallery walkways between the courts. Who would have believed that 48 hours before? ...

Cars were parked all over the lush green grass adjacent to the regular tennis and platform tennis courts. Hundreds of galvanized spectators packing the bleachers along the side and end of the championship court buzzed with anxiety between points and roared in unison at the end of particularly lengthy rallies or

134

lightning-fast exchanges. It was pulsating "paddle" at its finest, and in its finest hour!

While the first-time fans marvelled at the players' seemingly effortless screenplay and agile footwork, the more knowledgeable gallery members couldn't help but appreciate the competitors' concentration, patience, shotmaking abilities and subtle changes of pace that are invaluable attributes when playing top-flight, winning platform tennis.

It was a final round worthy of the exquisite setting. The "kids" from New Jersey were neither overawed by their formidable opponents nor the pressure of the ever-grinding cameras. They seemed to be relaxed and courageously parrying the very best offensive shots their older and more experienced opponents could offer.

After losing the first two sets—the second one was a heartbreaker since they were far ahead at one point—the Baird brothers rallied to win the third one in a spine-tingling tiebreaker, 7-6. John Mangan, with the score at six games apiece and four points each in the tiebreaker, lashed out with one of his big forehands and drove the ball beyond the baseline. It was one of the gutsiest shots I have ever seen in watching championship platform tennis. He and Kingsbury had a match point, a single point away from an all-expense paid trip to Europe—and rather than playing it safe, he went for the Big One.

John and Bob fought tenaciously for the fourth set. They played as though they realized their youthful adversaries would most likely sweep them off the court if the match went to five. Performing almost flawlessly, they took the final point, game, set, and match by winning the fourth set six games to three.

The gallery showed its appreciation and

admiration with an ear-shattering eruption of loud and sustained applause. I sincerely doubt if Jay Michaels, in his production of the final film for television, will have to dub in spectator sounds as he originally believed would be necessary. All the appropriate sights and sounds were present that afternoon, and they were genuine.

Awards ceremony. John Mangan and Bob Kingsbury (left) listening to Sea Pines developer, Charles Fraser(right) congratulate them on their victory.

We were told to keep speeches very brief for the awards presentation ceremonies. The participants in the Vat Gold Cup had to rush to make the last plane home. In addition, television producers have never been too enamored with the ritual of awarding trophies at the end of any athletic contest (with the exception, perhaps, of the Olympics or Wimbledon).

Charles Fraser had flown back from Haiti especially to attend the final. After being introduced, he compared John and Bob's victory with Arnold Palmer's comeback in the 1969 Heritage Golf Classic and Stan Smith's memorable conquest of Rod Laver in the CBS televised tennis matches—both events, coincidentally, having taken place at Sea Pines.

He then said, "But *never* have I seen a more thrilling athletic contest or sport than the one we have just seen these fine players put on." He turned and pointed at me. "Several months ago this crazy guy Squires tried to talk my association and me into installing a few of his courts down here. We hedged because we really didn't believe the game could be played in warm weather. Then he brought up a very good point. Dick reminded us why people everywhere are frantically seeking various forms of exercise. Sure, it's for enjoyment, but what they really want out of their participation in sports is to sweat, to cleanse and streamline their bodies. I think today's match showed all of us that platform tennis is a game to be played the year-round—in any kind of weather. We plan on installing several more courts at some of our other developments ..." I hardly heard the rest.

Replicas of the large, permanent Vat Gold Cup were presented to the champions and smaller ones to the elated Bairds. A horde of professional and amateur photographers jammed the court and were taking pictures of the awards ceremony. It was as if Chris Evert had just come off the hallowed Centre Court at Wimbledon. The little-known, esoteric sport of platform tennis had, at long last, taken a giant step toward emerging from behind the manicured hedges.

That evening as the National Distillers' corporate jet started racing down the Savannah Airport runway, I pressed back against the overstuffed, comfortable seat and gazed out the window. The plane lifted off effortlessly and climbed almost noiselessly into the clear, black night. An uncontrollable smile spread across my face as we sped skyward. The smile was one of tasty smugness born out of the sheer satisfaction of knowing a job had been done right and well. Everyone had profited—the players, the corporate sponsors, and the sport of platform tennis itself.

The accomplishment was not in itself the end of something finite, but, perhaps, the miniscule beginning of something possessing infinite potential.

chapter 18
Potential markets for the game

Author's Note: Even though my unwavering enthusiasm for platform tennis back in the 1960s was bound to influence my opinions when I wrote this chapter, I still feel paddle courts are a marvelous recreational facility for practically any place.

One of the problems, however, with the installation of courts is that the vast majority of Americans are still not familiar with the sport and its many appeals. They have never even heard of the game, let alone ever played it—or even seen it played.

For paddle courts to be installed at all the places mentioned in this chapter, the sport has to become better known. For example, resorts won't have courts put in until enough visiting guests ask, "Where are the platform tennis courts?" In other words, there has to be a demand.

The same is true of schools and colleges. Wealthy alumni might donate a couple of courts to their alma mater, but if the kids never go on them it's sort of a waste of money. So much for intercollegiate competition taking place at least in the foreseeable future. Not enough youngsters have been introduced to the joys of paddle by the time they go off to college.

Another negative factor that now has to be considered is the cost of a court. The price tag has quadrupled in the past 20-plus years. They are now *more expensive to build than most tennis courts.*

Because the wires are an integral part of the game and a playing surface, paddle courts are not deemed to be a "safe" recreational facility for public parks. They are easily vandalized. Someone snips the screening and you no longer have a playable court.

So, until this wonderful game is given more national exposure on television (and it is not easy to televise), until a court is installed at the White House, until some famous person takes up and extols the virtues of the sport, until there is a pro tour and prize money and people willing to pay to see the game played by the best, until it is considered to be a game that can be enjoyed the year-round, platform tennis just will not be the popular athletic amenity at all the places I wrote about. And that's a lot of untils!

RESORTS

Certainly resorts, including lavish hotels and motels, ski areas, hunting lodges, etc., represent a potential market for the introduction of the game as an added recreational facility. With shorter work weeks and more time for travel, stress-free sport and fun, these resorts will inevitably be competing for a greater portion of the dollars spent by people in "pursuit of happiness." The owners of these holiday paradises and hostelries have come to the realization that they not only should, but must offer their guests a great deal more than delectable viands, clean sheets and cable TV. Conveniences, social activities and recreational facilities are no longer additional "fringes"—they are absolute necessities if the resorts are to attract the trade.

Many owners and managers now are beginning to

learn they must remain open the *year-round* in order to show a profit. Ski areas are attempting to promote themselves as summertime places to stay in. Pools, golf courses, and tennis courts have been added.

Platform tennis courts are certainly a facility that, if properly introduced and promoted, will lure people to a particular place in preference to others that might not have courts. The decade of the 1970s (and the '90s!) should show a swing of the pendulum back toward the family, and an eagerness to return to genteel, participatory sports. The violence of football, the sedentary state of spectating, the slowness and "apartness" associated with golf, the ennui of swimming, the continuing growth in popularity of regular tennis and an increasing concern for physical fitness and healthful exercise, should all be important factors in making platform tennis a welcome pastime during the forthcoming years.

The small space required for a court is also appealing to resort owners who have to figure every acre (just as supermarket managers compute dollars by square feet of shelf space) as revenue-producing units with which to outdo and outsell their competition.

In addition, little or no maintenance is required to keep the courts in top playing condition—less than five percent upkeep annually. With ever-increasing labor costs, platform tennis courts certainly involve a great deal less servicing than either swimming pools or, for that matter, tennis courts.

Although I may be accused of being prejudiced, I truly believe there is no better recreational facility for a resort, hotel or motel to offer its guests. The installation of paddle courts, accompanied by a well-planned program and some publicity, can mean more rooms sold, more incremental profits to the establishment—with a relatively minimal investment required.

SCHOOLS AND COLLEGES

Just think of all those learning institutions located in Northern climates that have a huge number of tennis courts available for a season that lasts all of two months—April and May of the school year, and, perhaps, a few weeks in the fall. What an utter waste. The main beneficiaries of these courts are the "townies" who use them during the summer months when the students are away on vacation.

Platform tennis courts, on the other hand, could be utilized for a minimum of six months. In addition, many schools and colleges that have traditionally been all-male have now become co-educational. The co-eds find themselves with meager athletic facilities. (Not as true today!) Wouldn't paddle courts be the perfect sports facility for them?

If Harvard were to install, say, four courts, Yale and Princeton would almost immediately erect six to eight, respectively. It is not hard to envision intercollegiate competition taking place with the top event being *mixed* doubles. Why not?

While athletic directors have to spend much of their time building up strong football teams to placate the old grads, most of them are primarily concerned with ways of cajoling the majority of students to participate in some—or any—sports activity at all. Intramural, non-varsity athletic programs for the "unnatural" athlete-undergrads are really what most athletic directors are dedicated to establishing. Broad participation is their aim.

142

Certainly platform tennis is the ideal game for the non-athletic, as well as natural athlete. The added expense of a coach is not necessary, as it is the only racquet game I know of where anyone can pick up a paddle and have fun (without becoming totally frustrated) from practically the first moment.

I can imagine myself someday in the future sitting in the stands watching the finals of the U.S. Intercollegiate Platform Tennis Doubles Championships. Wouldn't that be great! And I suspect the complexion and style of the game will have changed considerably. The play will undoubtedly be far more aggressive, with a premium on lightning-like reflexes, speed of foot, and a greater majority of hard hit, offensive shots off the wires.

And then when the collegians are graduated from their respective academic institutions and enter the business or professional world, they will take their sport with them, and Lord help the club they join if "paddle" is not one of its leisure-time activities!

MUNICIPALITIES

Most cities throughout the country are presently concerned with two basic and omnipresent problems:(1) The young people in their streets, many of whom seem apathetic toward recreation and healthy physical exercise and,(2) a shrinking percentage of the city's annual budget being allotted to recreation at a time when funds are most needed.

Even though the majority of public servants are responsible and concerned individuals, they have, by circumstance and necessity, come to believe that public recreational facilities have to be at least self-sustaining financially. It would be wonderful if the city swimming pool, municipal golf course and tennis courts could be offered free for all citizens, but with ever-increasing costs, this is no longer possible.

Any city or town in the U.S. would find it hard to select a more ideal athletic facility than platform tennis courts. Courts would keep the parks open and utilized the year-round. The lights for night play would make the parks safer during the evenings. The structures occupy little space and require minimum maintenance. No other racquet and ball pastime offers richer rewards for family participation during long, wintry evenings.

When funds are unavailable in the city budget, some communities have screened the local town folks to ascertain the amount of interest they have in the sport. Nominal financial commitments have been obtained in the form of $50 to $100 per season family memberships. If enough money is raised, it becomes possible to obtain the required balance from a local bank— especially if the bank president or chief loan officer happens to like the idea of public paddle! Many people who are concerned about their personal physical fitness and well-being will be more than willing to pledge a reasonable sum at the beginning of each season because of the many joys the game offers them. It does not take too many such commitments to accrue enough dollars to afford public paddle courts.

Figuring 50 families per court, a couple of hundred families can easily purchase three to four courts—then a full-fledged paddle program is off the ground, paid for and supported by the people who will use and enjoy the new facility the most.

COUNTRY CLUBS

Most private golf and tennis clubs today find themselves unhappy victims of the current depressed economy. (Same is true in the 90s.) Many of their members have had to resign because they no longer can afford to belong. Other members who continue to belong have had to cut back drastically on their club activities and participation.

Combine this with rising labor costs, plus the difficulty of hiring good, reliable help at any price, has really put the squeeze on innumerable private clubs throughout America.

What is the solution for these clubs? How are they going to survive, let alone thrive? The answer is easy and inexpensive—wintertime platform tennis.

Increased club usage means increased revenues that can more than offset the additional expenses involved in keeping the club facilities open. If need be, a separate, winter platform tennis membership can be instituted at a reasonable rate.

Platform tennis is unique from the standpoint that practically anyone—young or old—can have fun playing it while learning. People who cannot play tennis become completely addicted.

The deck is 30'x60', or one-quarter the area of a regulation tennis court. When space is at a premium, portable decks can be installed in the fall right on the tennis courts, dismantled and stored in the spring.

As the game continues to expand into new areas, and many new players are exposed to its delights, undoubtedly more team matches will be instigated—thus creating an increased amount of activity at the clubs. Women, especially, find themselves using the

145

club facilities during the week with greater frequency. Paddle courts are a no-lose facility for country clubs everywhere.

RECREATIONAL COMMUNITIES

In the future many corporations will be investing heavily in land to develop recreational, leisure-oriented communities. Their marketing efforts and planning will be slanted toward convenience, the second home, and "buy your own home and rent it out when you are not using it." The advertising message will be the promise of pollution-free air, the serene, carefree life, days and nights of fun and healthy recreation. Such idyllic meccas will fill a timely need and stir the imagination. Add concern for health and fitness, and the installation of platform tennis courts makes a good deal of sense.

The architects and planners of these developments from the earlier planning stages wouldn't think of excluding such basic facilities as tennis courts, a swimming pool, perhaps (if the amount of land allows) a golf course, and shuffleboard or horse shoes for the elderly. Why not paddle courts?

If these same planners can somehow become familiar with platform tennis and all the "goodies" the game offers its participants, many would specify paddle courts in the original plans. Why? The courts consume little valuable space, require a relatively small investment and scant maintenance, and can and will be appreciated and used by all members of the family in almost any kind of weather day or night. I defy you to designate any other form of recreation that offers so much.

146

ROOFTOPS

In crowded major cities, the only valuable unutilized space remaining nowadays is rooftops. In-town city dwellers could find enjoyment, camaraderie and a healthy release from everyday problems and stress during the evening or over weekends by joining a club that offers rooftop platform tennis. Installation would not be cheap, but it is possible. Platform tennis courts can be squeezed in anywhere—even be a money-maker for investors in such a project.

CORPORATE HEADQUARTERS

Company morale and employee fitness represent key concerns for present-day American business. A well-organized recreational/ fitness program for companies is a primary objective of the Human Resources department of all progressive firms. Many corporations across the country have already made the exodus to suburbia where land is plentiful and the employees do not have to spend a great deal of their day commuting to work. Appealing and well-planned recreational programs and facilities breed a feeling of esprit and "belonging." They also keep the employees in reasonably good physical shape, which means fewer lost man hours due to sickness. Platform tennis courts represent an excellent facility to offer these employees. Industrial leagues could become a reality and popular. They precipitate company loyalty and enthusiasm.

OTHER SITES FOR PADDLE

Where else can platform tennis be played? How about mobile home campsites and trailer-home-parks? Private homes, YMCA and YWCA, hospitals and nursing homes, golf driving ranges and pitch and putt golf courses are "ripe" for paddle. Prisons (don't laugh!), health spas and sanatoriums, beach clubs, amusement parks are also potential sites for commercial paddle. Courts can be an added and appropriate amenity at indoor tennis clubs and neighborhood semi-private sports complexes.

Get the idea? There really aren't too many places where platform tennis courts should *not* be installed. It truly is a great sport with broad appeals for *everyone.*

chapter 19

Implementing a successful platform tennis program

A uthor's Note: My friend, Les Overlock, is no longer organizing paddle events or playing the game he truly loved. He died several years ago. What a fun gentleman he was, and his genuine fondness for the sport was contagious. I cannot think of too many other individuals who cajoled more people out onto the boards, and then got them hooked for a lifetime. I miss him.

No matter how contagious a sport platform tennis is, it still takes an *organized program* to put it over when new courts are installed. The following suggestions are written primarily for the Platform Tennis Committee and its chairman at a club (located in cold-weather areas) where two or more courts have recently been erected. The identical procedures, however, hold true where courts are installed in public parks, condominiums, schools and colleges, resorts or hotels, or even at a service base in, say, Nome, Alaska. Someone has to see that a program is developed to encourage participation. It is a very rewarding assignment; once the program is implemented and under way it will grow and expand almost automatically because of the game's broad appeals.

Platform Tennis Committee

It is important for the new chairman to select eight to 10 committee members—preferably husband-wife combinations—who will inject their enthusiasm and energies into the "paddle program" for the entire season. Because the club is located in a cold-weather region, the first meeting for the committee should take place no later than the middle of August, as play traditionally commences around the latter part of October. Well before the official kick-off of the season, a schedule of events and tournaments should be mailed out to the membership.

Inaugural Exhibition

To help assure a propitious start-up, an inaugural exhibition/clinic given by four first-rate players is desirable. The tyros and totally unknowing members will see firsthand how the game should be played. These exhibitions, if properly promoted and performed, are a marvelous way to engender enthusiasm and encourage participation among the members of any group.

Tournaments and Other Events

At the August committee meeting a list of tournaments for the entire season should be planned. Care should be taken that these do not conflict with other invitation tourneys to be staged at nearby clubs. Assign a specific committee chairman for each event. Some of the following "friendly" club tournaments and events should be considered for any paddle program:

Mixed Member/Member Scrambles

This is an ideal event to kick off the new season.

Anyone interested in playing the game can participate and have fun in this handicap-type tournament. Players (male and female) are classified or ranked by the committee chairman "A" to "C", and the best (A) men are matched up with the weakest (C) women, and vice versa. The entries are then carefully seeded so that the stronger teams do not meet each other in the early rounds.

To further increase interest and participation it is worthwhile to have both *Consolation* (all first-round losers) and, when there are many entries, *Reprieve* (those teams eliminated in the second round) championships.

The most successful handicapping method being employed to date is the so-called "Sliding Zero-to-Six System." Each team is carefully rated from zero (like scratch golfers, these are the most skilled teams), two, four or six, with six being the weakest.

If the team is rated, say, six, this means they can, at their own choice and when it is most timely during the match (although they must announce to their opponents that they are taking their points *before* a game begins), decide *when* they wish to take their six points—which is tantamount to one and one-half games.

For example, if a six-rated team is vying against a two-rated team, the six, or underdog, can award itself four points (the difference between the two teams) whenever they feel it will mean the most to them. Only the team with the higher handicap can decide when to use its points. If this team happens to be leading in games in the first set, 5-4, obviously they will then take their four points, which means they automatically win the first set, 6-4.

Now comes the great equalizing aspect of this type

of handicapping. At the end of the first set, the winning team receives two fewer points for the next set. In the above illustration, the underdog team won the first set, and, therefore, has only two points they can utilize in the second. If the favored (two-rated team) had won the first set, in spite of having to "give away" four points to the opposition, they would have to award six points during the second set. The same "sliding handicap" system would also hold true if a third or deciding set should be required.

It is truly amazing how well this system works, and it precipitates a great deal of fun and many close, exciting matches. It is obviously very important that the players and the team be rated by a person(s) who is quite familiar with the players' skill levels.

Mixed Member-Guest

This event is usually staged during the post holiday "dog days" of January when people have recuperated sufficiently from Christmas and New Year's and are ready for a social/athletic weekend. In this format, club members invite partners from other clubs. This is usually a straight (no handicap) tournament, but Consolation and Reprieve matches assure broad participation and adequate exercise for everyone.

Frequently an integral and pleasant part of this type tournament is the Saturday night dinner dance at the host club. This enhances the conviviality of the event, and also enriches club revenues. (One club in Connecticut, which has had platform tennis courts for only three years, recently made a study of the financial impact of the game on their club revenues. Much to the pleasant surprise of everyone, they discovered that 68 percent of the income generated during the slow months of October through March was directly attributable to platform tennis.)

Men's Member-Guest

Same as mixed doubles, except the women spend the weekend watching and rooting for their husbands. Cocktail parties and a club dinner dance enhance the camaraderie of such a tournament. Ditto and vice versa for Ladies' Member-Guest.

Club Championships

These are traditionally held toward the end of the season. Plaques should be purchased for either the clubhouse or warming hut, and the names of the winning teams inscribed on them with the appropriate year. Photographs of the finalists can be framed and hung to enhance the prestige and tradition of these events.

Husband-Wife Club Championship

Otherwise known humorously as "The Divorce Open," or "The Longest Weekend," this annual contest can be the most fun of all, despite its being a great test of even the happiest marriages. But in spite of the steely glares, the tears, and moments of strained silence, serious marital break-ups have not been reported (as of this writing). The winning combination can "stand tall" with the knowledge that they have truly *earned* their trophies.

Friday Night Paddle Parties

At least once a month during the winter, couples who have been bitten by the platform tennis bug should be encouraged to stage Friday night round-robin events. If the number of couples exceeds eight, it is best to divide the teams into two or more flights. Each team plays, say, eight games against all the other combinations in its group. The teams with the greatest number of games won in their respective flights then meet and play a one-set final.

An important part of such social competition is an open-fire barbecue or cookout with an abundant supply of liquid refreshments both hot and cold. Such an evening can be inexpensive and a marvelous way to culminate a hard week and embark on a fun weekend.

Junior Championships

If the kids (18 and under) at the club have an opportunity to play (their parents frequently have hogged the courts), they too should be encouraged to compete in a club championship against their own age group.

The ideal time to have this event—if eight or more teams can be fielded—is during the Christmas or mid-winter holidays when they are home and on vacation and can play during the week.

Parent-Child Tournaments

This event is always enjoyable and a special treat for the youngsters. It is best to schedule it during the holidays when the kids are home and available.

Special Club Invitationals

Many clubs have become regular stopovers for the better men and women players during the season. The dates selected for invitational tournaments should fall on approximately the same weekend each year—in other words, they become traditional events.

The teams invited are oftentimes the best players available, and watching them play affords club members the opportunity of viewing the game as performed by "experts." Such events arouse the interest of the entire club, and improved play invariably occurs because the novices attempt to emulate the "pros." Quite often a major social function is scheduled around such an event and the visiting players attend. During the evening the inevitable question is asked of the competitors by the members: "Say, how would you like to play with me in our Member-Guest Tournament next year?"

Ladies' Day

One morning a week—usually Wednesdays—should be designated strictly for the nonworking ladies. Round-robin competition, coffee and doughnuts, perhaps even luncheon, provide the women with a pleasant and healthy mid-week outlet.

Junior Clinics

Several clubs have inaugurated a development program for the youngsters who much too rarely get the opportunity to play. A few of the better players in these clubs have scheduled early Saturday morning 8 to 9 clinics for interested adolescents in the age bracket of 10 to 16. These clinics have been tremendously successful and well attended.

Family Days

As platform tennis becomes more and more popular, Sunday afternoons from 2 to 5 are frequently reserved strictly for family play. This is a wonderful idea as it is a fabulous family participation sport. These sessions also afford the youngsters with another opportunity to improve.

Inter-Club League Matches

As platform tennis expands to neighboring clubs, ladies' and men's inter-club rivalries should develop and be encouraged. These are friendly team matches that occur during the season and usually involve "home" and "away" matches against each participating club. Such reciprocity affords everyone the opportunity of entertaining each other's team and enjoying each other's club facilities.

Miscellaneous

All club final-round matches for all tournaments should be umpired. This officiating lends a good deal of stature to the events, and is greatly appreciated by players and spectators.

Every institution, whether it be a club, resort or condominium, should automatically join the American Platform Tennis Association just as soon as the courts are put in. By joining, they will keep abreast of the latest doings in the sport, receive tournament notices, and feel part of the game.

A bulletin board strictly for platform tennis should be acquired and displayed in an obvious place either in the clubhouse or warming hut. Upcoming events, sign-up sheets for tournaments, playing rules, announcements, etc., will be posted for members. It is a good way to communicate with the players and keep the action going.

Tournaments should be publicized at least three weeks in advance of the date, and the particular chairman of the event must be prepared to make many phone calls to remind and encourage the players to enter.

Entry fees for all these tournaments and events mentioned should be established at a modest rate, but should be adequate to cover the cost of balls, trophies, refreshments and whatever. More elaborate, optional events that are part of a tournament (e.g., a formal dinner dance) are charged separately.

It is always worthwhile to present some sort of prizes for tournaments. Even the rather inconsequential social round robins should offer recognition to the winners–if only something as simple as a few new balls. The more prestigious championships should offer functional prizes and have the particular title of the event, plus the year, engraved on them.

Monies for such "spoils" can be obtained either at the beginning or close of the season by soliciting the members to contribute to a "Platform Tennis Prize Fund." Donations are voluntary, but if a person hasn't contributed and wins a tournament, he or she does not get a trophy. This system has proven successful in raising funds voluntarily!

When paddle courts are being considered, it is best, whenever possible, to install a minimum of two courts. A single court can frequently discourage people from taking up the game because of the difficulty in getting a reserved time slot. Two courts, set side by side or end to end, breed camaraderie and bring out the innate amenities that are so much a part of this game. A warming hut is also highly desirable and should be in the original plans.

Installation of Courts

There is a definite procedure to follow when consideration is being given to installing paddle courts.

Choosing the proper site is most important. The area selected should be esthetically appropriate.

Consideration must be devoted to the convenience factor; i.e., how far from the clubhouse and the parking lot? Because lights for night play are a must, picking a site within close proximity to a power source is vital. How accessible will the paddle area be in case of a heavy snow fall? The site selected should be large enough to accommodate additional courts, as well as a warming house. It should also be accessible for ease of construction, and if the area is a residential one, thought has to be given to any potential problems and complaints that could occur from neighbors.

After the site has been determined, it is important to obtain bids from bona fide contractors who are *experienced* in platform tennis court construction. Sometimes clubs and institutions ordering courts hire a local carpenter . . . and invariably live to regret it. (Author's Note: When Les wrote these words, courts were made of wood, not aluminum!)

After a method of financing the courts has been resolved, the new court-owner-to-be should apply for a building permit, if this is required. Be sure to stipulate a completion date for construction with your contractor, and give the court-builder as much lead time as possible.

By adopting the above suggestions, and by adding your own novel ideas and activities, you should be well on your way to the successful implementation of a popular platform tennis program.

Leslie C. Overlock

chapter 20

The paddle

Author's Note: Because of the development of space-age materials and technology, the design of the tennis racquet has radically changed and improved during the last 10 years. Tennis racquets have become lighter, stronger and more powerful. Also more expensive!

Though stiffer than their predecessors, they better absorb the jolt when the racquet meets the ball. New strings, combined with these new frames, make the racquets more responsive. Hitting the ball with more authority and more spin are pluses. Whether these new tennis racquets materially change the game—for better or for worse—is yet to be proven.

Thanks primarily to Marcraft Recreation Corp., which has designed and manufactured the great majority of platform tennis paddles for the past three decades, an evolution similar to the tennis racquets has taken place. Paddles today are more responsive, softer and lighter. How this affects on-court play will be interesting to observe.

Early platform tennis paddles (1950s), made by Dalton Manufacturing in Pennsylvania, used lacquered, laminated white-maple marine plywood. They had a sturdy U-shaped steel binding around the perimeter of the head. Essentially they offered but two models, a 16 ounce and a 13 ounce for men and women, respectively. A pattern of drilled holes cut down on wind resistance and allowed

the players to apply some spin to the balls. They were decent paddles, although, in time, the metal binding frequently came loose and they "rattled" upon impact with the ball.

To eliminate the rattle , Marcraft engineered an

extruded aluminum channel shaped like an "M" with a barbed-center member. This protective metal piece around the edge of the head fit flush with the paddle face and, therefore, did not tend to loosen with contact with the deck and screens. Few people mourned the passing of the distinctive Dalton rattle!

During the 1960s another Marcraft innovation was introduced—the open-throated paddle. This produced lighter-headed paddles that allowed the players to accelerate the head faster on their strokes. The result was added power. In addition, the metal throat absorbed more of the shock and vibration from ball contact.

Eventually fiberglass replaced the laminated wooden face, which further reduced vibration and increased power. This material was more flexible, resisted warping, and was more durable.

Several years ago Marcraft introduced thin layers of graphite fibers into the body of their paddles. Graphite has high-tensile strength that produces quick flex. This trait, in turn, produces power with less effort. The graphite fiber also uniformly distributed the force of the ball striking the paddle across the entire paddle face, which created the happy combination of increased power and more precise control.

Wood layers were replaced by light, dense, durable and highly resilient polymer layers. They compressed and returned more quickly than the wood layers. Again, more power.

Then Marcraft, observing what was happening to the design of tennis racquets, created mid-size models—or expanded face paddles. By augmenting the face width, the hitting area, as well as sweet spot, were enlarged by 30 percent. This made it easier to strike the ball for players of all skill levels.

Then, naturally, the widebody or "thick paddle" was invented by the people at Marcraft to cushion the jolt that occurred when the rigid paddle contacted the heavy, spongy ball. So-called "tennis elbow" had become an unwelcome endemic malady to platform tennis, and this painful condition deterred many people from playing the game. The double and triple thick paddles manufactured with low-density shock absorbing materials effectively ameliorated this undesirable situation. With greatly reduced shock and vibration being absorbed in the body of the paddle, the result, once again, was better response and touch.

The latest Marcraft innovation is even lighter, more resilient polymers being employed to produce ultra wide-bodied paddles (22 millimeters thick), which are about 30 percent thicker than the previously thickest models. By utilizing new materials, extremely powerful but highly controllable paddles can and will be manufactured. They will be 2 to 3 ounces lighter than any previous models. This, in turn, creates a paddle that is more wieldable.

Yes, indeed, the platform tennis paddle has come a long way in looks, performance and durability since the days of the old Dalton. With new materials being created, there is no reason to believe that future progress and new, better paddles won't be conceived and made. And Marcraft will, hopefully, continue to be pioneers in the constant improvement of paddle performance.

Duffy Lautz is president of Marcraft Recreation Corporation, located in Passaic, N.J.

chapter 21
The court

The construction of the first platform tennis court in 1928 was more of a happenstance than a planned event. In the comfortable setting of Scarsdale, N.Y., two executives decided they wanted to exercise outdoors throughout the winter and so they designed and built a wooden platform in order to be above the confines of the wet and difficult snow conditions.

They chose wood because it was the least expensive material. They surrounded the court with chicken wire to prevent the ball from rolling down the hill and being difficult to retrieve. From this very simple and almost naive beginning, platform tennis courts have evolved to elaborate and well-engineered structures made completely of aluminum.

In the more than 60 years since that first primitive structure, the playing surface and surrounding screening have become infinitely more sophisticated. In addition, a variety of lighting systems were introduced to extend play into the evening hours.

From 1928 to 1968, platform tennis grew from a small neighborhood club activity into an accepted and desirable sport in many of the most prominent country and golf clubs throughout the Northern parts of the United States. During that period, the sport was always played on courts made totally of wood. The wood source was Douglas fir, usually from the West Coast. In some cases the wood was pressure-treated to extend its life span and slow down the rotting process.

The Problems with Wood

The wood decks had two serious problems: The wood boards would rot over time and, because of the short length of the boards, the butt joints appeared in inconvenient areas of the playing surface often resulting in uneven ball bounces. Approximately 30 years ago, R. J. Reilly Jr., Inc. developed a 30-foot deck board that would eliminate the joints throughout the playing surface. All joints would occur just underneath the net. This became the accepted standard of court construction and improved the playability of the deck.

The wood surfaces, however, still rotted. They would check; they would cup; layers of paint would build up and then, because of moisture trapped in the wood, the paint would peel leaving crevices and indentations resulting in bad ball bounces. The yearly resurfacing required to keep the deck surfaces in playable condition would accelerate in cost as these

aging concerns would develop with time.

Each year the number of courts being built increased as the sport gained in popularity throughout the country. In the late '60s and early '70s it received a fair amount of national publicity in newspapers, magazines, and even a few television programs. The originators probably never dreamed such exposure would come to a game they developed in their backyard. Along with the increase in popularity of the sport, the expectations of the players and the quality of play rose to higher and higher levels.

It was evident during this growth period that the difficulty of maintaining a wood playing surface had to be overcome. During this time experimentation was done with many other types of wood to try to improve upon and overcome the rotting characteristics of the softer Douglas fir. Experiments included a very unusual wood from British Guiana called greenheart, and a wood that could last in salt water for up to 100 years without showing any sign of rot. Unfortunately, these types of wood had other problems that affected the quality of the playing surface and the ball bounce, and thus were not acceptable substitutes for the Douglas fir.

Carpeting was tried in several applications as another method to overcome the problem of repainting surfaces. Unfortunately, the use of carpeting only increased the rate at which the wood would rot.

The other medium that still lingers on is that of a plastic surface on top of wood. The problem is this surfacing only covers up and makes invisible the rot that is going on underneath. In fact, in any area where rain, moisture and evening dew or dampness are factors, such courts become extremely slippery and even dangerous to play on.

The Switch to Aluminum

A medium had to be found that would be economically feasible, provide a desirable playing surface and yet overcome the ever increasing problems with a wood deck. The material R. J. Reilly eventually chose was aluminum. Reilly spent a full year working with engineers developing what has become the mainstay in court construction for the past 20 years– the all-aluminum court.

The immediate and very obvious advantages of aluminum were recognized by most people; the lack of any deterioration due to the fact that aluminum does not rust or rot, nor does it check or move. These factors overcame the two significant problems with the wood, the deterioration of the material and the lack of an even playing surface for consistent ball bounce.

The other significant advantage to aluminum is that it is a conductor of heat. This, in turn, enabled us to introduce a heat source underneath the deck to melt snow and ice before it could build up through the coldest months of the winter.

Aluminum did pose its own challenges. Play on an aluminum court was noisy. We were also initially unsure of how to fasten the boards so that they would give a solid rebound surface for the ball. Additionally, it was difficult to get the paint to adhere properly to the aluminum surface for a long period of time.

With continued research and field testing, Reilly has been able to overcome these factors and deal with them effectively and desirably. Noise has been reduced to a point where it is virtually unnoticeable. We have effectively addressed the challenge of solidly attaching the deck boards to the undercarriage. And finally, the adhesion of the paint to the deck surface has been resolved so that in some instances our paint surfaces

168

have lasted up to 14 years without any need for repainting.

The Benefits of Aluminum

Possibly the single biggest benefit of the aluminum court is that clubs with active memberships can guarantee (with a heating system) that Saturday morning play will not be delayed by a frozen or iced-up playing surface, thus allowing people with busy schedules to fit in their favorite pastime.

With the more than 100 APTA-sanctioned tournaments played during the cold months of the year, aluminum provides much greater control and predictability than in past years when wood courts were the rule. Heating the aluminum deck to remove snow and ice provides the additional advantage of eliminating abusive shoveling. This shoveling can, over time, remove a fair amount of the surface that provides the traction for players in wet and slippery weather. It is not unusual to see players playing on a dry, snowless aluminum surface during a snow storm. They simply turn on heaters and melt the snow as it falls on the deck surface.

Reilly has perfected another great benefit to the all-aluminum court: A screening system that provides consistent ball bounce. When properly installed with the correct tension springs added, this system enables the screens to remain tight for many years, thus requiring virtually no maintenance. Long-term, consistent screen tension was never possible with wood because of the method of fastening screens to the wood members. It has also been observed that the screening, when attached to the aluminum superstructures, has a considerably longer life span.

The final benefit of the aluminum superstructure is

the allowance of screen shots that rebound further into the court, thereby enabling players with lesser skills to keep the ball in play longer than they would be able to on softer screens attached to wood superstructures.

Installing an aluminum platform tennis court can be costly initially. A large amount of aluminum must be used to manufacture a court able to withstand the rugged use that a platform tennis court is exposed to. The benefits of the aluminum court, however, make it a wise investment. The initial high cost of installation is offset by the durability of the court resulting in dramatically lower yearly maintenance costs. This is in considerable contrast to clay tennis courts and swimming pools where the cost and time of daily or weekly maintenance is a large factor. An aluminum platform tennis court can go many years without requiring resurfacing or maintenance other than shoveling snow. Unlike a swimming pool or tennis court, an aluminum platform tennis court also has the unique and desirable attribute of being relatively effortless to move to another location because it is quite easily disassembled. These benefits, combined with the life span of the court, have made it a vastly improved investment over the wood court.

Unusual Sites and Installations

With the advent of the aluminum court, it became possible to install platform tennis courts at sites that were not feasible for wood courts. These sites include some unusual locations. R. J. Reilly installed the aluminum court for the New Canaan, (Conn.) annual tournament that was held for a number of years on the New Canaan High School gym floor. The reason for the indoor installation was to avoid changing weather conditions and, in turn, seat large crowds. This

170

enabled the event to be used as a fund-raiser for the town athletic program. At the peak of the pro-tour activity, Reilly actually installed a court on a Park Avenue sidewalk in the heart of Manhattan. Over a period of several days we exhibited the top players in match-like conditions; an event that included the televising of some of the activity.

R. J. Reilly did a similar temporary installation of two courts in the middle of the stadium at Forest Hills on top of its grass courts. This was again to stage a tournament with the top players with none other than the famous sportscaster, Howard Cosell, announcing the various rounds of the tournament.

In the heart of Manhattan, 51 stories high, another court was installed by Reilly on a permanent basis. This court continues to receive active use for those willing to venture that high into the atmosphere. We have also suspended several courts over swimming pools for winter use, which were then taken down during the summer. We have installed courts in garage roof-parking structures. They have often been temporarily installed on tennis courts. They have been placed on hillsides where one end of the court will be as much as 20 to 25 feet in the air. Courts have been built over streams and swamps; out in the middle of dry, arid areas in warm weather locations including

The Argentine version of paddle tennis. Literally thousands of courts have been built just during the last 10 years–both indoor and outdoor.

Bermuda, Florida, southern California and the Carolinas. They have been built as far north as Alaska and various sections of Canada. And, presently, R. J. Reilly, Jr., Inc. has developed a paddle center in northwest Montana where although the snow has been as high as four feet above the deck level, it has never impeded play due to a new engineering approach.Today's court owners range from homeowners to 'arge companies such as IBM. And between that range are small tennis clubs, hunt clubs, neighborhood groups, embassies, condominium installations, resort facilities, and high school and college courts. While the primary owners have consistently been golf and country clubs, there is no limit to the who or where of the platform tennis court location.

People, Places and Seasons

The growth of platform tennis has traditionally been in the New York metropolitan area. When players from this area move, they manage to take the game with them and this has been the main cause for the growth of the sport to other parts of the country. Currently, the largest active playing area in the country, outside of the New York metropolitan area, is in and around Chicago. It is interesting to analyze why this has occurred. Of course, population and availability of financial resources and club locations have a great deal to do with it. The other, more subtle factors relate to the nature of the game itself. It's a game that is usually picked up by tennis players, but is certainly not limited to tennis players. In the colder areas, such as the Midwest, winter is a time when people look for things to do outside. For many people platform tennis has filled this need quite adequately.

Summer, for most of us, comes and goes very quickly with many activities to fill our time. Winter often lacks the same amount of activity. Tennis, golf, swimming, boating, hiking, and so many of our warm weather sports, shut down in early September or certainly by October. People in the colder climates find that their platform tennis season can begin comfortably in October and extend well into March and, in many cases, all the way through April.

Clubs and Warming Houses

In our involvement with all types of platform tennis facilities over many years we have noted two factors that have contributed significantly to active play in metropolitan areas: The development of leagues and the proper design and construction of well-located "warming houses." League play has the benefit of guaranteeing match play that is both competitive and social. The competition is effectively controlled by having a variety of levels of play so that people can play at their comfort level. And the sociable nature of platform tennis is enhanced by the comfortable warming house that enables players to watch others as well as enjoy the conversation and presence of fellow members.

The design and placement of warming houses and warming huts, is quite critical. Their location should actually enhance play. If they are built either too close or too far from the courts, they can be unproductive. Consideration should also be given to the addition of bathroom facilities and even kitchen appliances (i.e., refrigerator, sink, cooking facilities) to encourage its usefulness.

We have also observed a third very helpful factor: Club programs seem to be most effective when run by an active and enthusiastic teaching pro. The pro can help those interested in improving their game as well as organize round robin, parent/child, member/guest, club championships or tournaments that stimulate and continue to develop interesting play for the members.

Location

The location of the courts is critical to their acceptance by players. Most of the play will occur in colder weather. Some of the play will occur when the ground is covered with snow. For these reasons, courts should be constructed close to parking and clubhouse or home access. Wind direction and sun should also be considered.

Courts look best when kept as low as possible to the ground. Reilly has developed a technique for keeping the deck level with the ground and still enabling the surface to be cleared of snow and ice. This new engineering will be significant in the acceptance of platform tennis court installations in areas previously ruled out for aesthetic reasons. The result of the lower court is greater visibility of court play as well as easier access for players.

Lighting and Heating

Lighting and heating systems vary in design and price. Generally the simpler the system, the better it will perform. We designed the quartz-halide lighting system in 1960. We later developed the fluorescent lighting system. With time we found that the higher installation cost of the fluorescent system was compounded by the higher maintenance cost of lenses and bulb deterioration, as well as cleaning cost. We also found the fluorescent system experienced loss of light intensity with time and cold weather. These factors, coupled with 80 percent player dissatisfaction as compared to quartz or halide lighting, directed us back to improving our original and simpler quartz system. We did this by adding two 1500-watt fixtures at the net line, providing a total of six fixtures instead of four.

Similarly, we designed several heating systems over the years. Most recently we have perfected a system that melts snow and ice more efficiently than any other in a short period of time. It is also an easier system to service and maintain.

The fuel cost for properly heated courts should range from $200 to $400 per court each season. Lighting should cost between one and two dollars per hour per court depending on the cost of kilowatt hours in a given area.

Snow removal should be done with plastic push shovels. The wetter the snow, the more damage can occur to the aggregate surface. Be very careful in scraping the painted surface. Wet snow adds considerably to the downward forces exerted by the leading edge of the shovel. Lowering the handle is important as well as pushing small quantities. The most important factor is removing the snow as soon as a snow storm has ended. A light snow of several inches can be removed by one person in 15 minutes by shoveling or flipping a switch to run the heaters.

Cost

Maintenance costs for properly designed and installed all-aluminum courts are minimal. No more than $2,500 should be spent to resurface a court every four to six years. A yearly fine-tuning of gates, snow boards and screen tensioning may also be necessary. The cost should be no more than $100 to $200, plus travel cost depending upon court location. Owners should not attempt to repaint an aluminum deck surface without hiring the very best contractors in the platform tennis court business. Accepting a low price or hiring a questionable contractor will cost much more in the end and can result in considerable damage to the deck surface. An inadequately painted surface can even expose the owner and contractor to liability lawsuits that can be very costly.

The cost of a properly designed, manufactured and installed platform tennis court typically ranges from $30,000 to $40,000. Variables such as lighting and heating systems and court location will affect the final price.

The cost of purchasing a platform tennis court should be divided by a factor of 30, which equals its expected life span. This will determine the annualized cost of such an installation over the 30-year period. The additional maintenance and operational expenses are virtually nullified by their proximity to our inflation factor and ever decreasing dollar value. Once divided out, the yearly expense of $1,000 to $1,400 for such a facility should be divided further by 20. Assuming that the average court is used throughout a six- to seven- month season by 20 active players the yearly total cost is approximately $50 to $70 per player per year. If each player uses the court twice a week for 90 minutes, the total would be as low as $1 per hour.

Platform Tennis as a Resort Sport

In Whitefish, Mont., next to Glacier National Park, the Big Mountain Ski Area and beautiful Whitefish and Flathead Lakes, Reilly has constructed a platform tennis complex designed to provide year-round play and extensive instruction. The climate in this area is quite desirable for platform tennis thanks to low summer humidity, moderate winter temperature and the lack of heavy rain. As a destination resort area, it offers every outdoor activity, including the very best of downhill and cross country skiing, fly fishing, rafting, alpine hiking, golfing and horseback riding.

The resort can accommodate groups of 12. Platform tennis court activity combines individual and group lessons as well as supervised play. Play is customized to the needs, desires and time constraints of the participants. Bookings can be arranged by calling 406-862-2233.

Summary

Platform tennis has seen a tremendous evolution over the past 64 years. It has gone from a primitive backyard aberration to an internationally recognized sport utilizing sophisticated technology while providing competitive fun for people of all ages. We are proud of our contributions to platform tennis and will continue to search for and develop innovations to improve and enhance this great sport.

Richard J. Reilly, Jr. is owner and founder of R. J. Reilly Jr., Inc., the first and largest manufacturer of platform tennis courts. Dick has been influencing the sport of platform tennis since 1959. Thanks to his efforts we now play on safe and efficient aluminum courts.

Located in Brewster, N.Y., R.J.R., Inc. has, since its inception, built more than 2,600 courts in 41 states and 11 foreign countries. The aluminum court he created is undoubtedly his greatest contribution to the sport he has helped·promote and foster for 30-plus years.

chapter 22
Etiquette

By Robert A. Brown

A uthor's Note: *My longtime friend, Bob Brown, a stalwart at the Fox Meadow Club both on and off the court, is responsible for writing (and re-writing) the "official" rules of etiquette. He couldn't have been a better choice, for a gentleman he most certainly is.*

Copies of "Etiquette," as well as the "Official Rules of Platform Tennis," are available by sending your request to: The American Platform Tennis Association, P.O. Box 901, Upper Montclair, N.J. 07043.

If you are going to play any sport often and/or even seriously, it is a good idea to become familiar with its playing rules and its more subtle guidelines relative to on-court demeanor. The latter, etiquette, while far more loosely interpreted than the strict rules of play, is, however, equally important.

INTRODUCTION

Platform tennis, often referred to as "Paddle" for short, is a keenly competitive sport and one in which, by tradition, good sportsmanship, integrity, and respect are key elements. It is a game that is played for fun, but there is also an active winter tournament circuit. The game is played in accordance with the Official Rules of Platform Tennis as published by the American Platform Tennis Association.

The main purpose of this chapter, however, is to discuss the *etiquette* of platform tennis play. Etiquette is an area in which, unlike rules that are generally more specific, there may be differences of opinion, or judgment may have to be exercised. Because platform tennis is attracting many new participants, the APTA believes it desirable to provide these guidelines on the etiquette of the game. In doing so, it is recognized that etiquette does have its "gray areas." Therefore these comments are offered, not as hard and fast rules, but as suggested guidelines of behavior. In any case, it is hoped that the tradition of the game will be maintained through a continued high degree of sportsmanship and mutual respect, and that this booklet may assist in furthering that tradition by offering worthwhile suggestions on personal behavior while playing this rewarding game.

I. LINE CALLS

In matches where there are no linesmen, the general rule is that all lines are called by the receiving team; i.e., you call lines on your side, the opponents call lines on their side. Each side should, obviously, call the ball in or out honestly and without regard to the play situation. The decision of the team whose responsibility it is to make the call is final.

The following refinements are suggested:

1. If an "out" call is not promptly made, the ball is considered "in" and play should continue.

2. On service, line calls may be made by either member of the receiving team. If an "out" call is made, play should stop. If there is a disagreement between the receiving partners as to whether the service was good or out, a "let" should be played, regardless of whether the service was returned in or out of play.

3. During play, if a player makes an "out" call on a ball that the player could otherwise return, and the player stops play, but his partner thinks the ball was in, a "let" should be played.

If an "out" call is made on a ball that neither partner could retrieve, but the caller's partner disagrees and believes the ball was "in," the point should be awarded to the opponents.

4. Players may assist their opponents with "out" calls in the opponents' court, if requested. They should also call against themselves any ball that is *clearly* out on the opponents' side of the court, if not called by the opponents.

5. A certain amount of friendly kidding about opponents' line calls is inevitable. But etiquette dictates that the opponents' line calls are to be respected and considered final. In the end, "questionable" calls will usually balance off between the two sides.

6. If there is uncertainty about a line call, as stated in the Official Rules, "Any doubts should be resolved in favor of the opponents."

7.When coaching your partner to let a ball drop rather than hit it, try to use commands such as "bounce it!" or "drop it!" rather than "out!" so as not to confuse your opponents, who may think you are making an "out" call.

II. FOOT-FAULT

The foot-fault is the rule that demands the greatest amount of self-control by the server. Seldom will fellow players advise another player that he is foot-faulting for fear of "offending." Yet, if in serving, he is stepping on or over the baseline before striking the ball, he is breaking the rules just as seriously as if he faults on the service by hitting the ball into the net or out.

Many players may not know they are foot-faulting. This is because, in serving, they make a slight movement of the forward foot, which is legal, but in doing so they step on or over the line. A player can find out if he is foot-faulting by asking a fellow player to observe his service. Conversely, a polite comment to another player, who himself will not ask, may not be out of order. One subtle way to handle this is to ask a player if he would like to have you call his foot-faults during his practice serves.

The server is "on his honor" not to foot-fault; therefore all players should exercise the self-control necessary to stay behind the line while serving. Apart from the rule-breaking and etiquette aspects of foot-faulting, linesmen may call foot-faults in the semi-finals and final of major tournaments, and any player who is in the habit of foot-faulting regularly may have a difficult time adjusting to a correct service procedure under the pressure of tournament competition. The usual result is that he will lose points on called foot-faults or serve a higher percentage of faults in trying to adjust to a legal service.

So, in this area above all others, etiquette says that players must exercise the greatest degree of self-control in order not to break the rules and/or offend others. Practice serving, legally, and check with others by asking that your service be watched.

III. "LET" BALL ON SERVICE

The server's partner is closest to the net and in the best position to hear a "let." He should call it promptly, loud and clear. It is also permissible for either member of the receiving team, if he believes he heard the ball tick the net, to promptly call a "let," in which case the service should be played again.

IV. BALL HITTING PLAYER

If a ball touches any part of a player's body or clothing (including any part of the hand) either before landing or hitting the screen on the player's side, or after landing fairly in the court, it results in loss of point. Even if the player is standing outside the boundaries of the court, the point is lost if the ball strikes him before landing on the deck or hitting a screen. Often a ball striking a player just barely grazes his clothing or hair. It is good etiquette for the player himself to declare that the ball touched him and award the point to the opponents.

It is not good etiquette for any player to declare that the ball hit an opponent and thereby "claim" the point. He may, if he wishes, politely ask if it did, but the determination of whether or not the ball hit the player is that player's to make, and his integrity and decision in the matter should be respected.

V. THE "TICK"

A ball that is "ticked" is barely grazed with the paddle, and often when this happens only the player who "ticks" the ball can hear or feel it. It is good etiquette for the player doing so to promptly declare that he touched the ball and award the point to the opponents.

It is poor etiquette for opponents to declare that a player "ticked" the ball and claim the point. The best person to determine whether the ball was ticked is the player himself, and it is good etiquette to respect his integrity and decision.

VI. TOUCHING THE NET

Touching the net with any part of the body or the paddle during play is loss of point. A player touching the net should promptly declare that he did so and award the point to the opponents.

On rare occasions, a ball driven by a player into the net will force a loosely strung net to strike the paddle of the opposing net man who may be crowding the net. If this occurs, it is loss of point for the net man, as he touched the net before the ball fell to the deck to conclude the point. (Moral of the story: Always tighten the lower net strings.)

VII. THE "CARRY" AND THE "DOUBLE" HIT

The "carry" is difficult to define, but the word fairly suggests what occurs, and it is illegal. It is an excessively long contact between the paddle and the ball, as distinct from a cleanly struck shot. The carry is illegal because it could give a good player an unfair advantage. The carry can inadvertently occur in almost any playing situation, but one of the most common is when two teams are having a rapid exchange of volleys near the net and a player, in moving backward while receiving and attempting to return a shot, unintentionally "catches" or "cradles" the ball on his paddle. If in his judgment he has "carried" the ball he should declare it and award the point to the opponent.

A "double hit" can occur in this situation and in the more difficult wire shots. In this version of the "carry," the player in attempting to return a shot hits the ball twice in quick succession. It is rare, but it does happen. And as it is illegal it should be promptly declared by the player and the point awarded to the opponents.

184

VIII. DOUBLE BOUNCE

If a player knows that the ball has bounced twice before he hits it, he is honor-bound to call "not up" on himself and award the point to the other team.

IX. REACHING OVER THE NET

It is against the rules to reach over the net to strike a ball unless it has first landed in the striker's court. An over-the-net violation should be called by the violating player or his partner as a matter of good etiquette. It is not good etiquette for the opponents to make that call and claim the point.

X. RETURN BALL TO THE SERVER

When a point is completed, if the ball is lying on your side of the court and your opponent is serving, it is good etiquette to pick up the ball and either give it to your opponent's net man, who can give it to the server, or gently bounce the ball to the server in his next service position, waiting a moment if his back is turned before "feeding" it to him.

All too often players simply kick or push the ball in the opponents' direction or arbitrarily hit the ball just anywhere over to the other side. This makes the server chase the ball, it is discourteous, and it results in a slow-moving game.

It is good etiquette to do your part by picking up the ball and getting it to the server in an easy and accommodating manner. If everyone does this it will be easier on you when your turn comes to serve.

Finally, above all, resist the temptation of venting aggravation at missing an easy shot by slamming the ball about the court after the point is lost.

XI. THE WOMAN IN MIXED DOUBLES

This can be a sensitive subject. However, no document on etiquette would be complete without touching at least briefly on it. Specifically the question is how the man should play against the woman in an opposing mixed-doubles team, particularly if the woman is the weaker of the two partners. There are two schools of thought. The first, which is more often applied in friendly games, says that the man should be "gentlemanly" by not driving the ball hard at the woman at net, or in returning her serve, and should not work her corner disproportionately. This does have the advantage of balancing play between opposing partners, it is "gentlemanly," and it avoids the label of "picking on the woman." In an otherwise close contest it can also lead to losing the match.

The other school of thought says that a team is a team, sex makes no difference, and the normal strategy to beat a team that may be unbalanced is to play the weaker partner. If that partner happens to be a woman, so be it. And if the woman does not like that, she need not play (or can get better).

Both viewpoints have merit and both have their strong advocates. It is not uncommon to see a "double standard" practiced, with the first school of thought being applied in friendly, social games where winning or losing may be unimportant, or even in an unbalanced tournament match; and the second standard being applied in a keenly contested tournament match. We believe it best to leave the choice to one's personal discretion.

XII. ON LOSING

It is much more difficult to be a gracious loser than a winner. One should be gracious in either case—but try particularly hard to be so in losing. Congratulate your opponents, wish them well, live with it, and strive to improve so you can be a gracious winner.

XIII. GOOD MANNERS

In closing, a few "do's and don'ts" on good manners are included, although most of these suggestions are obvious:

1. Be punctual. The game requires four players, and it is good etiquette to be on time and not inconvenience the other players by being late.

2. Bring a ball.

3. Don't use bad language during play (or, keep it to yourself).

4. Don't bang the paddle against the net, the side screening, or the deck as an outward expression of self-dissatisfaction.

5. As a courtesy, don't deliberately wear yellow clothing with the intent of making the yellow ball more difficult for your opponents to see.

6. Be complimentary of good play by both your partner and your opponents.

NOTE: Within this text, the use of any particular gender is intended to include the other gender.

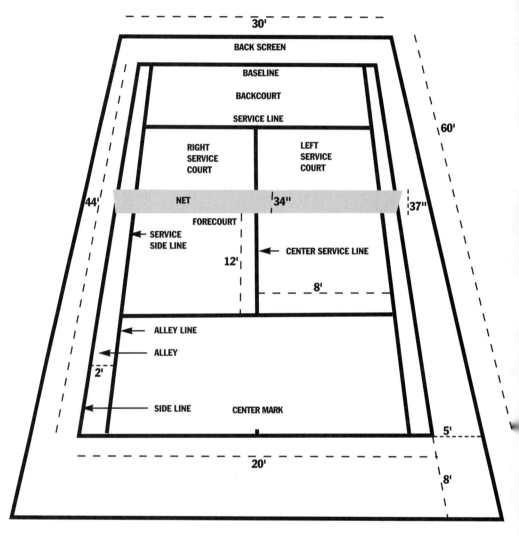

**Dimensions of Platform
Tennis Court Deck**

chapter 23

The APTA's official rules of platform tennis

RULE 1

Dimensions and Terminology of the Court

The *court* is a rectangle 44' long and 20' wide, laid out on a *surface* with a playing area 60' by 30' which is enclosed by a *screen* 12' high. The screen is held taut by a *superstructure* around the perimeter of the deck. Screens are made of 1" hexagonal galvanized wire mesh.

The court is divided across the middle by a *net*, the ends of which are attached to *posts*. The posts are 37" high and 18" outside the court (acceptable tolerance ± 6"). The height of the net at the posts is 37" and at center is 34". The net is held down taut and adjusted for height by a vertical *center strap* 2" wide.

The lines at the ends of the court, parallel to the net, are called *baselines.* The lines at the sides of the court, perpendicular to the net, are called *sidelines.* Two feet inside the sidelines and running parallel to them for the length of the court are the *alley lines.* Twelve feet from the net on either side and running parallel to it from alley line to alley line are the *service lines.* The segments of the alley lines between the service lines and the net are called the *service sidelines.* The area between the net and the service lines is divided in half by a line perpendicular to them. This line is called the *center service line.* Each baseline is bisected by an imaginary extension of the center service line called the *center mark.* The center

191

mark appears as a line 4" long extending into the court at right angles to and touching the baselines.

The area between the baseline and the service line is called the *backcourt*. The area between the service line and the net is called the *forecourt*, which in turn is divided into two *service courts*, left and right. The area between the side line and the alley line is called the *alley*.

All lines are customarily 2" wide and all measurements are made to the outside of the lines from the net or the center of the center service line. This line is in both service courts and is itself centered on the imaginary center line of the court. All lines are within the court.

There is a space of 8' between each baseline and the *back screen*, and a space of 5' between each side line and the *side screen*. These spaces are part of the playing area, but they are not part of the court.

On either side of the court, or on both sides, an access door is cut into the superstructure. The door is located near the center of the court.

RULE 2

Court Fixtures
Court Fixtures are the net, the posts, the cord (or metal cable) that holds up the net, the band across the top of the net, the center strap, the screens, the snow boards, the superstructure, the doors, the lighting poles and lights, any crossbeams or corner supports within the enclosure, and, when they are present, the umpire and his chair.

RULE 3

The Ball and the Paddle
The ball is a rubber ball with either orange or yellow

flocking, conforming to APTA specifications for diameter, weight, bounce and other standards as set forth in Appendix A.

The paddle is 17 inches in overall length with a playing area 10 3/8 inches long and a handle 6 5/8 inches long. The paddle is perforated with a number of 3/8 inch holes. The surface of the paddle must be flat and the finish smooth. APTA paddle standards are set forth in Appendix B.

RULE 4

Use of Ball and Paddle
Only one ball shall be used continuously during each set unless otherwise specified by the tournament committee. Server may not substitute another ball during an unfinished set without the permission of tournament officials, nor may server hold two balls while serving.

A player may not carry a second paddle during play, although it is permissible to use both hands on the paddle and to switch the paddle from hand to hand in the course of play.

RULE 5

Singles Match
The rules are the same except for the following: in singles, the game is played within the standard singles court, two serves are allowed and no-ad scoring is used. The no-ad game point is served into whichever service court the receiver chooses.

The Hi-Bounce ball is recommended for singles.

RULE 6

Choice of Sides and Service

The choice of sides and the right to serve first or to receive first are decided by toss, which is generally accomplished by spinning the paddle.

The team that does not toss has the right to call the toss. The team winning the toss has the following options:

(a) The right to serve first, in which case the other team has the right to choose from which end of the court to receive;

(b) The right to receive first, in which case the other team has the right to choose from which end of the court to serve;

(c) The right to choose the end, in which case the other team has the right to elect to serve first or to receive first, and

(d) The right to require the other team to make the first choice.

RULE 7

Server and Receiver

After the toss has been concluded, the teams take their places on opposite sides of the net. The member of the serving team who elects to serve first becomes the *server.* The member of the receiving team who elects to play the right court becomes the first *receiver.*

The server must deliver service from a position behind the baseline and between the center mark and the sideline, diagonally crosscourt from the receiver.

The receiver may stand wherever he pleases on his own side of the net, on or off the court. Likewise the server's partner and the receiver's partner may take any position they choose on their own sides of the net, on or off the court.

The server alternates serving, first from behind his own right court into the receiver's right service court, then from behind his own left court in to the receiver's left service court, and so on. Members of the receiving team alternate receiving service.

If the server serves from behind the wrong court and his mistake is not discovered until the point has been completed, the point stands as played, but thereafter the server must serve from the correct court according to the score. If the server serves from behind the wrong court and the mistake is detected by the receiving team after the service has been delivered and that team does not attempt to return the service, the server loses the point.

The ball served must pass over the net cleanly and hit the deck within the proper service court before the receiver may return it. Receiver may not volley the serve, i.e., strike the ball before it has bounced. If he does so, receiver loses the point outright.

RULE 8

Delivery of the Service
The service is delivered as follows: The server takes an initial position behind the baseline and between an imaginary extension of the center mark and the sideline, as described in Rule 7. The server then projects the ball by hand into the air in any direction, and before it hits the ground strikes the ball with his paddle. At the moment of impact the service delivery is completed.

NOTE: The serve may be delivered overhand, underhand or sidearm as the server chooses. There is no obligation on server's part to inform receiver as to his intention, and server may vary his type of delivery.

RULE 9

Only One Service
Only one service is allowed. If the service is a fault, the server loses the point. If the service is a let, the server serves the point again.

RULE 10

Fault or Out
The serve is a fault if:
(a) The server does not take a legal position as described in Rules 7 and 8;
(b) The server commits a foot-fault (see Rule 11);
(c) The server misses the ball completely in attempting to strike it;
(d) The ball does not land in the proper service court;
(e) The ball served hits the server's partner, and
(f) The ball touches a court fixture other than the net, band or center strap before it hits the deck. If it touches any of the above fixtures and then lands within the proper service court, it is a let (see Rule 13).

COMMENT: It is customary for the receiving team, especially receiver's partner, to determine whether the serve is a fault by reason of:
(a) The ball's having landed outside the proper service court or

(b) The Server's having violated the foot-fault rule. The first such call of a foot-fault on each server in a match not being officiated shall be a let. After his "grace fault" it is loss of point.

Under tournament conditions, if there are linesmen, they assume the responsibility for calling all foot-faults. At any time in any round of a tournament match any player is entitled to request a foot-fault judge and/or linesmen.

A *ball in play* (other than a serve) is out if it does not land within the court on the proper side of the net after either crossing the net or touching the net, post, cord, band or center strap.

NOTE: Since all parts of the lines bounding the court are deemed to be within the court, a ball that touches any part of a line is good.

The usual procedure is for the receiving team to make line calls on its own side of the net in matches in which there are no linesmen. Any doubts should be resolved in favor of the opponents.

RULE 11

Foot-fault
The server shall, throughout delivery of the service, up to the moment of impact of paddle and ball:
(a) Not change his position by walking or running;
(b) Not touch, with either foot, any area other than that behind the baseline within the imaginary extension of the center mark and the sideline.

NOTE: The server shall not, by the following movements of his feet, be deemed to "change his position by walking or running:"

(1) Slight movements of the feet that do not materially affect the location originally taken by him;

(2) An unrestricted movement of one foot, so long as the other foot stays continuously in its original contact with the deck;

(3) Leaving the deck with both feet.

RULE 12

Receiving Team Must Be Ready

The server must not deliver his serve until the receiving team is ready. If the receiver makes any attempt to return the ball, he is deemed to be ready. Also, if the receiver attempts to return the ball it is deemed that his partner also is ready.

If the receiver says that he is not ready as a serve is being delivered, the serve shall be played again, provided the receiver does not attempt to return the ball. In such case, the receiver may not claim a fault should the serve land outside the service court.

RULE 13

A Let

In all cases where a let is called, the point is to be replayed.

The *service* is a let if:

(a) It touches the net cord, center strap or band and then lands in the proper service court;

(b) After touching the net, band or center strap it touches either member of the receiving team or

198

anything they are wearing or carrying before hitting the deck, regardless of where they might be standing, on or off the court;

(c) It is delivered when the receiving team is not ready (see Rule 12).

A *ball in play* is a let if:

(a) It hits an overhanging obstruction such as a tree limb or a crossbeam;

(b) The ball becomes broken in the course of a point;

(c) Play is interrupted by an accidental occurrence such as a ball from another court bouncing into the court.

NOTE: In any situation during the play of a point when a let may be called, if the player who could call the let does not do so immediately and permits play to continue, that decision is binding on his team. It is not reasonable to opt not to call a let, strike the ball for loss of point, and then ask for a let to be called.

RULE 14

Serve Touching Receiving Team

If the serve touches the receiver or the receiver's partner or anything they are wearing or carrying before the ball has hit the deck, the server wins the point outright, provided the serve is not a let as described in Rule 13 (b). This ruling applies whether the member of the receiving team is hit while he is standing on or off the court.

RULE 15

When Receiver Becomes Server
At the end of the first game of a set the receiving team becomes the serving team. The partners decide between them who will serve first in each set. The order of service remains in force for that entire set.

RULE 16

Serving or Receiving Out of Turn
If a player serves out of turn the player who should be serving must take over the serving from the point that the mistake is discovered. All points stand as played.

If an entire game is served by the wrong player the game score stands as played, but the order of service remains as altered, so that in no case may one player on a team serve three games in a row.

If the receiving team receives from the wrong sides of their court (as established in their first receiving game of the set) they must play that entire game from the "wrong courts" but must revert to the original sides of their court the next game they are receivers.

RULE 17

Ball Remains in Play
Once a ball is put into play by service, it remains in play until the point is decided, unless a fault or a let is called.

EXPLANATION: A player may not catch a ball that appears to be going out-of-bounds and claim the point. The ball is in play until it actually hits the screen on the fly, or bounces on the deck. A player catching or

200

stopping a ball and calling "out" before the ball is legally out loses the point for his team.

RULE 18

Loss of Point
A team loses the point if:

(a) The ball bounces a second time on its side of the net, provided the first bounce was within the court;

DISCUSSION: Sometimes it is difficult to determine whether a player attempting to retrieve a ball, especially a drop shot that has bounced once and is about to bounce again, actually strikes the ball before it bounces the second time. Propriety dictates that the player attempting to hit the ball is honor bound to call "not up" if he feels the ball did in fact bounce twice. A player who has any doubt in this situation will ask the nearest opponent, after the point has been decided, "Was I up?" If the opponent says no, the point should be conceded.

(b) A player returns the ball in such a way that it hits:

(1) The deck on the other side of the net outside the side lines or baseline;

(2) Any object, other than an opposing player, on the other side of the net outside the sidelines or baseline;

(3) The net, post, cord, band or center strap and does not then land within the court on the other side of the net.

(c) A player volleys the ball and fails to make a good return, even when standing outside the court:

EXPLANATION: A player standing outside the court volleys at his own risk. It is not proper to volley the ball and simultaneously call it "out," for if the ball is volleyed it is in play.

(d) A player touches or strikes the ball more than once in making a stroke, or makes overlong contact with the ball (making both a double hit and a carry illegal);

(e) A player volleys the ball before it has crossed over to his side of the net, i.e., reaches over the net to strike the ball, making contact on the opponents' side of the net (See Rule 20b);

(f) A player is touched by a ball in play, unless it is a let service (See Rule 13b);

NOTE: It does not matter whether the player is inside or outside the court, whether he is hit squarely or his clothing merely grazed, or whether the contact is accidental or purposeful. If a ball touches anything other than a player's paddle it is loss of point.

(g) A player throws his paddle at the ball in play and hits it;

(h) A player bounces the ball over the screen and out of the enclosure or into a lighting fixture, whether or not the ball rebounds back into the court, and

(i) A player or anything he wears or carries, touches the net, post, cord, band or center strap, or the court surface on the opponents' side of the net, within the boundary lines, while the ball is in play.

NOTE: If the point has already been concluded it is not a violation to touch any of these fixtures. Also, if in rushing to retrieve a drop shot, a player's momentum carries him past the net post onto the opponents' side of the net, this is not loss of point unless the player actually steps inside the opponents' court or interferes with one of the opponents. Mere physical contact with an opponent is not loss of point unless such contact hinders the opponent.

202

When a player is standing at the net and the opponent hits the ball into the net in such a way that it pushes the net against his paddle or his person, the net player loses the point. It does not matter that the ball was not going over the net. The net player loses the point because he made contact with the net while the ball was still in play.

RULE 19

Ball Touching Court Fixtures
If the ball in play touched a court fixture (as defined in Rule 2) after it has hit the deck within the boundaries of the court, the ball remains in play and may be returned, so long as it has not hit the deck a second time on the same side of the net.

EXCEPTIONS: If the ball hits a lighting fixture, the point is concluded–loss of point for striker. If the ball hits a crossbeam it is a let.

In matches in which an umpire and an umpire's chair are inside the enclosure, a ball striking either the umpire or his chair prior to landing in the opponents' court is loss of point for the striker.

RULE 20

Good Return
It is a good return if:
(a) The ball touches the net, posts, cord, band or center strap and then hits the deck within the proper court;
(b) The ball, served or returned, hits the deck within the proper court and rebounds or is blown back over the net, and the player whose turn it is to strike reaches over the net and plays the ball, provided that

neither he nor any part of his clothing or equipment touches the net, post, cord, band or center strap, or the deck within his opponents' court, and that the stroke is otherwise good (See also Rule 21 Interference);

(c) The ball is returned outside the post, either above or below the level of the top of the net, whether or not it touches the post, provided that it then hits the deck within the proper court;

NOTE: It is not a good return if the ball is hit through the open space between the net and the post.

(d) A player's paddle passes over the net after he has returned the ball, provided that the ball had crossed to his side of the net before being struck by him, and that the stroke is otherwise good.

RULE 21

Interference

In case a player is hindered in making a stroke by anything not within his control, the point is replayed.

CLARIFICATION: If a tree branch or a ball from another court should interfere with play, a let should be called immediately. However, if a player bumps into his own partner or is interfered with by a court fixture, that is not grounds for a let.

In the situation covered by Rule 20(b), if the player who is attempting to strike the ball is willfully hindered by his opponent, the player is entitled to the point by reason of interference, whether such interference is verbal or physical. However, if it is agreed that such interference was unintentional, a let should be called.

RULE 22

Scoring

(a) The Game:

The first point is called 15, although it is also commonly called 5.

The second point is called 30.

The third point is called 40.

The fourth point is Game.

When both teams score 15, or both score 30, the score is called "15 all" or "30 all."When both teams score 40, the score is called Deuce.

The next point after Deuce is called Advantage for the team winning it, thus Advantage Server (or more usually Ad In), if the serving team wins, and Advantage Receiver (or Ad Out), if the receiving team wins.

If the team with the Advantage wins the next point, it wins the game. If the other team wins that point, the score reverts to Deuce. This continues indefinitely until one or the other team wins two points in a row from Deuce, which wins the game. Zero or no points is called Love. A game that is won "at love" means that the losing team scored no points.

(b) The Set:

The team that first wins six games wins the Set.

However, the winning team must have a margin of two games, and a set played under the traditional rules continues until one team has such a two-game margin, e.g., 8-6 or 11-9.

A set that is won "at love" means that the losing team won no games.

When the game is 6-all, the APTA recommends the use of the 12-point tiebreaker (See Appendix C).

Tournament Committees should announce in the tournament rules whether the tiebreaker is to be played.

(c) The Match:
A match is best of three sets with a tiebreaker in all sets.

COMMENT: In matches played without an umpire, the server should announce the point scores as the game goes on, and the game score at the end of his service game. Misunderstandings will be averted if this practice is followed.

NUMBER OF SETS TO BE PLAYED IN DIFFERENT EVENTS

Junior Girls– Two out of three with tiebreaker in all sets.
Junior Boys–Two out of three with tiebreaker in all sets.
Women's Ranking Tournaments– Two out of three with tiebreaker in all sets.
Men's Ranking Tournaments–Two out of three with tiebreaker in all sets.
Women's National Championship– Two out of three with tiebreaker in all sets. Last set of finals played out.
Men's National Championship–Two out of three with tiebreaker in all sets. Last set of finals played out.
Mixed National Championship–Two out of three with tiebreaker in all sets. Final set of finals played out.

RULE 23

When Teams Change Sides

Teams change sides at the end of the first, third, fifth and every subsequent odd-numbered game of each set.

When a set ends on an odd total of games, e.g. 6-3, the teams "change for one"—that is, they change sides for one game, and then change sides again after the first game of the next set. When the set ends on an even total of games, e.g., 6-4, the teams "stay for one" and then change sides after the first game of the next set.

RULE 24

Continuous Play

Play shall be continuous from the first serve of the first game until the conclusion of the match, except:

(a) For rest periods permitted by tournament officials;

(b) When changing sides on the odd games, a maximum of one minute is allowed for players to towel off, change equipment, rest, etc.

(c) Play shall never be suspended, delayed or interfered with for the purpose of enabling a player to recover his strength or to receive instruction or advice. The umpire shall be the sole judge of such suspension, delay or interference, and after giving due warning he may disqualify the offender. No allowance may be made for natural loss of physical condition such as cramps, faintness or loss of wind. Consideration may be given by the umpire for accidental loss of physical ability or condition.

NOTE 1: In the event of an accident, a fall, collision with a net post, a sprained ankle, and the like, up to a 10-minute suspension in play may be authorized. A default will be mandatory if play is not resumed immediately after the suspension.

NOTE 2: If a player's clothing, footwear, or equipment becomes out of adjustment in such a way that it is impossible or undesirable for him to play on, the provisions in Note 1 shall apply.

CLARIFICATION: The intent of the Continuous Play Rule is to prevent unauthorized rest periods for players who are tired and to discourage stalling tactics for whatever purpose. In the event of an accident, the umpire or tournament chairman shall consider a temporary suspension of play.

If a match is adjourned for a legitimate reason, e.g., a sudden rainstorm, when the match is resumed (a) the teams are entitled to a full warmup and (b) the match must begin precisely where it left off, with the same game and point score, same server, same sides of the court, and same order of service.

RULE 26

Only One Hit

In the course of making a return, only one player may hit the ball. If both players, either simultaneously or consecutively, hit the ball, it is an illegal return and loss of point. Mere clashing of paddles does not constitute an illegal return, provided that only one player strikes the ball.

208

RULE 28

Balls off Screens

If a ball in play or on the serve hits the deck in the proper court and then touches any part of the back or side screens, or both screens, or the horizontal top rails, or the snow boards, it may be played, so long as it does not bounce on the deck a second time on the same side of the net before being hit by the player.

NOTE: A ball taken off the screen must be returned directly over the net into the opponents' court. It may not be caromed back indirectly by being hit from paddle to screen and thence into the opponents' court.

APPENDIX A
BALL PERFORMANCE STANDARDS AND ACCEPTABLE TOLERANCES

The APTA has established the following Performance Standards and Acceptable Tolerances for the ball.

The APTA reserves the right to withhold or terminate approval if the Association feels the Standards have not been met by a manufacturer, and to approve balls for sanctioned play as it sees fit.

I. *Bounce Test for Rebound*

(a) Balls conditioned at 70 degrees Fahrenheit for 24 hours, then dropped from 90 inches to a concrete slab and the rebound measured. Bounce to be measured from bottom of ball.

Acceptable tolerance

Rebound 43" thru 48"

II. *Weight Test*

70 grams thru 75 grams

III. *Diameter Test*

Measure diameter along two perpendicular axes of the ball. Both readings must be within tolerance.

Acceptable tolerance

Standard Diameter   2 1/2" ± 1/32"

APPENDIX B
PLATFORM TENNIS PADDLE STANDARDS AND ACCEPTABLE TOLERANCES

Standard

Tolerance

	Standard	Tolerance
Total Length	18 1/16" maximum	None
Thickness *(Including rim)*	5/16" maximum	
Handle Length	6 5/8" maximum	None
Width of Head *(At widest point)*	9 5/16" maximum	
Play Length *(Handle to outside edge of rim)*	10 7/16" maximum	
Bolts and Nuts	flat and flush *(Preferably concealed by grip)*	None
Holes-Number	87 maximum	
Holes-Diameter	3/8"	None
Edges-Shape	Square or rounded	None
Surface Finish	Smooth	None
Surface	Flat	None

APPENDIX C
THE APTA APPROVED 12-POINT TIEBREAKER FOR PLATFORM TENNIS

REVISED 12-POINT TIEBREAKER

At six games all, the players continue to serve in order and from the same side as before. *The server of the first point of the tiebreaker will serve only one point and that to the Ad Court.* Each player will then, in normal service rotation, serve twice; first to the Deuce Court then to the Ad Court. The single point served by the initial server of the tiebreaker results in an immediate change of sides and teams will continue to change sides in the normal pattern as if the server had served an entire game. First team to win seven points wins set, although if it be six points all, the team must win by two points in a row. The set shall be scored at 7-6. The team receiving service for the first point of the tiebreaker shall begin serving the next set from the opposite side from which it received the first point. The teams shall change sides after the first game.

Example:

North	A B
South	C D

A started serving the set from N side.
It's six games all and it's A's turn to serve again.

1) A serves *once* (Ad Court) from N side.
Change sides.
2) C serves twice from N side.*

(Deuce Court first; Ad Court second)
(3) B serves twice from S side.
(Deuce Court first; Ad Court second)
Change sides.
(4) D serves twice from S side.
(Deuce Court first; Ad Court second)
(5) A serves twice from N side.
(Deuce Court first; Ad Court second)
Change sides and repeat this order until one
team reaches seven points or wins by two points
after each team reaches six points.
(6) Team C-D starts serving next from N side.
(7) Teams change sides after one game.
*Assuming that C has been following A in service
order.

THE DETERMINING SET OF THE FINAL ROUND
OF EACH TOURNAMENT MUST BE PLAYED OUT
WITHOUT A TIEBREAKER (THIRD SET OF TWO
OUT OF THREE-SET MATCH, AND FIFTH SET OF
THREE OUT OF FIVE-SET MATCH).

If a ball change is called for on a tiebreaker game,
the change should be deferred until the second game
of the following set, to preserve the alternation of the
right to serve first with the new ball.

ADDRESS
AMERICAN PLATFORM TENNIS ASSOCIATION
P.O. Box 901
Upper Montclair, N.J. 07043

Phone: 201-744-1190

chapter 24
List of U.S. champions

NATIONAL MEN'S PLATFORM TENNIS CHAMPIONS

Year	Champions
1935	Clifford D. Couch, Jr./Sumner D. Kilmarx
1936	Harold D. Holmes/Richard G. Newell
1937	James N. Hynson/Charles M. O'Hearn
1938	James N. Hynson/Charles M. O'Hearn
1939	Clifford D. Couch, Jr./Sumner D. Kilmarx
1940	Witherbee Black, Jr./Paul de F. Hicks
1941	Joseph B. Maguire/Clifford S. Sutter
1942	Holbrook H. Hyde/Leland Wiley
1943	Charles M. O'Hearn/Donald M. White
1944	Holbrook H. Hyde/Leland Wiley
1945	Joseph B. Maguire/Clifford S. Sutter
1946	Joseph B. Maguire/Clifford S. Sutter
1947	John Grout/John R. Moses
1948	Clifford D. Couch, Jr./Charles M. O'Hearn
1949	Richard K. Hebard/Frederick B. Walker
1950	Clifford S. Sutter/Sidney B. Wood
1951	Richard K. Hebard/Frederick B. Walker
1952	Richard K. Hebard/Frederick B. Walker
1953	Frank D. Guernsey/W. Donald McNeill
1954	Frank D. Guernsey/W. Donald McNeill

1955	James M. Carlisle/Richard K. Hebard
1956	George R. Harrison/William E. Pardoe
1957	Frank D. Guernsey/John R. Moses
1958	James M. Carlisle/Richard K. Hebard
1959	William M. Cooper, Jr./James P. Gordon
1960	William E. Pardoe/George R. Harrison
1961	Richard K. Hebard/Alexander H. Carver, Jr.
1962	Richard K. Hebard/Alexander H. Carver, Jr.
1963	Richard K. Hebard/Alexander H Carver, Jr.
1964	Oliver A. Kimberly, Jr./David Jennings
1965	Thomas Holmes/Michael O'Hearn
1966	Edward L. Winpenny, Jr./Dick Squires
1967	Oliver A. Kimberly, Jr./David Jennings
1968	Bradley Drowne/William Scarlett
1969	Gordon Gray/Jesse Sammis III
1970	Gordon Gray/Jesse Sammis III
1971	Gordon Gray/Jesse Sammis III
1972	John Mangan/Robert Kingsbury
1973	John Mangan/Robert Kingsbury
1974	John Beck/Herbert FitzGibbon
1975	Keith Jennings/Chauncy Steele
1976	Steve Baird/Chip Baird
1977	Herbert FitzGibbon/Hank Irvine
1978	Herbert FitzGibbon/Hank Irvine
1979	Clark Graebner/Doug Russell
1980	Steve Baird/Rich Maier
1981	Steve Baird/Rich Maier
1982	Steve Baird/Rich Maier
1983	Steve Baird/Rich Maier
1984	Doug Russell/Robert Kleinert
1985	Steve Baird/Rich Maier
1986	Hank Irvine/Greg Moore
1987	Hank Irvine/Greg Moore
1988	Steve Baird/Rich Maier
1989	Steve Baird/Rich Maier
1990	Steve Baird/Rich Maier
1991	Steve Baird/Rich Maier
1992	Rich Maier/Robert Kleinert

NATIONAL WOMEN'S PLATFORM TENNIS CHAMPIONS

1935	Mrs. Henry B. Eaton/Mrs. Percival S. Fuller
1936	Mrs. Henry B. Eaton/Mrs. Percival S. Fuller
1937	Miss Sally Childress/Mrs. Oscar F. Moore
1938	Mrs. T. Edmund Beck/Mrs. C.H. Walker
1939	Mrs. T. Edmund Beck/Mrs. C.H. Walker
1940	Mrs. T. Edmund Beck/Mrs. C.H. Walker
1941	Mrs. T. Edmund Beck/Mrs. C.H. Walker
1942	Mrs. T. Edmund Beck/Mrs. C.H. Walker
1943-1948	*Omitted because of wartime travel difficulties.*
1949	Mrs. T. Edmund Beck/Mrs. Oscar F. Moore
1950	Mrs. Ronald Carroll/Mrs. August Ganzenmueller
1951	Mrs. T. Edmund Beck/Mrs. Oscar F. Moore
1952	Mrs. T. Edmund Beck/Mrs. Oscar F. Moore
1953	Mrs. T. Edmund Beck/Mrs. Oscar F. Moore
1954	Mrs. T. Edmund Beck/Mrs. Oscar F. Moore
1955	Mrs. Ronald Carroll/Mrs. August Ganzenmueller
1956	Mrs. Peyton C. Auxford/Mrs. William Koegel
1957	Mrs. Edmund A. Raymond/Mrs. John A. Schwable

1958	Mrs. Ronald Carroll/Mrs. August Ganzenmueller
1959	Mrs. T. Edmund Beck/Mrs. W. (Susan Beck) Wasch
1960	Mrs. T. Edmund Beck/Mrs. William Wasch
1961	Mrs. S. Warren Lee/Mrs. Charles Sager
1962	Mrs. Rawle Deland/Mrs. William Wasch
1963	Mrs. S. Warren Lee/Mrs. Bradley Briggs
1964	Mrs. S. Warren Lee/Mrs. Bradley Briggs
1965	Mrs. Rawle Deland/Mrs. William Wasch
1966	Mrs. Edgar Nelson/Mrs. S. Warren Lee
1967	Mrs. S. Warren Lee/Mrs. Charles Stanton
1968	Mrs. S. Warren Lee/Mrs. Charles Stanton
1969	Mrs. Charles Stanton/Mrs. S. Warren Lee
1970	Mrs. Charles Stanton/Mrs. S. Warren Lee
1971	Mrs. Joseph Dillenbeck/Mrs. Ronald DeBree
1972	Mrs. Joseph Dillenbeck/Mrs. Ronald DeBree
1973	Mrs. Joseph Dillenbeck/Mrs. Ronald DeBree
1974	Mrs. Shirley Babington/Mrs. Marti Cavanaugh
1975	Hilary Hilton/Annabel Lang
1976	Wendy Chase/Linda Wolf
1977	Louise Gengler/Hilary Hilton
1978	Louise Gengler/Hilary Hilton
1979	Yvonne Hackenberg/Linda Wolf
1980	Yvonne Hackenberg/Hilary Hilton
1981	Yvonne Hackenberg/Hilary Hilton
1982	Yvonne Hackenberg/Hilary Hilton Marold
1983	Pat Butterfield/Robin Rich Fulton
1984	Robin Fulton/Yvonne Hackenberg
1985	Pat Butterfield/Diane Tucker
1986	Pat Butterfield/Diane Tucker
1987	Pat Butterfield/Diane Tucker
1988	Connie Jones/Gerri Viant
1989	Bobo Mangan/Sarah Krieger
1990	Sue Aery/Gerri Viant
1991	Robin Fulton/Diane Tucker
1992	Sue Aery/Gerri Viant

NATIONAL MIXED DOUBLES
PLATFORM TENNIS CHAMPIONS

1935	Charles M. O'Hearn/Mrs. Percival S. Fuller
1936	Mr. and Mrs. Charles M. O'Hearn
1937	Mr. and Mrs. Charles M. O'Hearn
1938	Mr. and Mrs. Charles M. O'Hearn
1939	Mr. and Mrs. T. Edmund Beck
1940	Mr. and Mrs. Charles M. O'Hearn
1941	Clifford S. Sutter/Mrs. J.B. Maguire
1942	Paul de F. Hicks/Mrs. Burr Price
1943-1945	*This tournament was omitted because of wartime travel difficulties.*
1946	Lamar M. Fearing/Mrs. Oscar F. Moore
1947	Mr. and Mrs. Elwood T. Cooke
1948	*No record of a tournament for this year.*
1949	Mr. and Mrs. Ronald Carroll
1950	Mr. and Mrs. Ronald Carroll
1951	Mr. and Mrs. Ronald Carroll
1952	Mr. and Mrs. Ronald Carroll
1953	Richard K. Hebard/Mrs. T. Edmund Beck
1954	Richard K. Hebard/Mrs. T. Edmund Beck
1955	John R. Moses/Mrs. Frank Smith
1956	Richard K. Hebard/Mrs. T. Edmund Beck
1957	Richard K. Hebard/Miss Ruth Chalmers
1958	Edward L. Winpenny, Jr./Mrs. Edward A. Raymond
1959	George F. Lowman/Mrs. Peyton C. Auxford
1960	Clifford S. Sutter/Suzanne Sutter
1961	James P. Gordon/Mrs. S. Warren Lee
1962	James P. Gordon/Mrs. S. Warren Lee
1963	Richard K. Hebard/Mrs. S. Warren Lee
1964	A.H. Carver, Jr./Mrs. William Koegel
1965	William Pardoe/Mrs. S. Warren Lee
1966	Gordon Gray/Mrs. William G. Symmers
1967	Gordon Gray/Mrs. William G. Symmers

1968	Gordon Gray/Mrs. William G. Symmers
1969	Bradley Drowne/Mrs. S. Warren Lee
1970	John Mangan/Mrs. David Harris
1971	Oliver A. Kimberly, Jr./Mrs. Allan Hannas
1972	John Beck/Mrs. William Wasch
1973	Cecil North/Mrs. Raymond O'Connell
1974	Bradley Drowne/Mrs. Ronald DeBree
1975	Herb FitzGibbon/Mrs. Ronald DeBree
1976	Herb FitzGibbon/Mrs. Ronald DeBree
1977	Doug Russell/Hilary Hilton
1978	Clark Graebner/Louise Gengler
1979	Doug Russell/Hilary Hilton
1980	Doug Russell/Hilary Hilton
1981	Doug Russell/Hilary Hilton
1982	Doug Russell/Hilary Hilton Marold
1983	Tom Smith/Robin Fulton
1984	Tom Smith/Robin Fulton
1985	Tom Smith/Robin Fulton
1986	Greg Tully/Meri Lobel
1987	Jim Kaufman/Connie Jones
1988	Bob Kleinert/Muffin Slonaker
1989	Mike Gillespie/Gerri Viant
1990	David Ohlmuller/Patty Hogan
1991	David Ohlmuller/Patty Hogan
1992	Rich Maier/Robin Fulton

1992 National Mixed doubles titleholders Robin Fulton (left) and Rich Maier.

PATIENCE AND PRACTICE PAY DIVIDENDS

LOB OFTEN AND SMASH RARELY

ALWAYS GO TO NET BEHIND YOUR SERVE

TALK FREQUENTLY WITH YOUR PARTNER

FOREHAND IS MOST OFFENSIVE STROKE

OVERHEADS SHOULD BE SOFTLY HIT TO BACK CORNERS

RETURN ALL BALLS WITH A PURPOSE

MAKE "FRIENDS" WITH THE SCREENS

TEAMMATES SHOULD BE TOGETHER AT THE NET OR ON BASELINE

ERRORLESS PLAY IS MORE EFFECTIVE THAN POWER PLAYS

NET CONTROL WINS MOST MATCHES

NEVER CHANGE A WINNING STYLE

INTRODUCE FRIENDS TO "PADDLE"–IT'S A WAY OF LIFE

SINGLE SERVE CALLS FOR SPIN, NOT SPEED

Notes